T0034367

A Cross in the Heart of God

A Cross in the Heart of God

Reflections on the Death of Jesus

Samuel Wells

CANTERBURY
PRESS
Norwich

© Samuel Wells 2020

First published in 2020 by the Canterbury Press Norwich
Editorial office
3rd Floor, Invicta House
108–114 Golden Lane
London EC1Y 0TG, UK
www.canterburypress.co.uk

Canterbury Press is an imprint of Hymns Ancient & Modern Ltd
(a registered charity)

Hymns Ancient & Modern® is a registered trademark of
Hymns Ancient & Modern Ltd
13A Hellesdon Park Road, Norwich,
Norfolk NR6 5DR, UK

All rights reserved. No part of this publication may be reproduced,
stored in a retrieval system, or transmitted,
in any form or by any means, electronic, mechanical,
photocopying or otherwise, without the prior permission of
the publisher, Canterbury Press.

The Author has asserted his right under the Copyright, Designs and
Patents Act 1988 to be identified as the Author of this Work

British Library Cataloguing in Publication data

A catalogue record for this book is available

from the British Library

978 1 78622 293 0

For Robert

There was a cross in the heart of God before there
was one planted on the green hill in Jerusalem.
And now that the cross of wood has been taken down,
the one in the heart of God abides,
and it will remain so long as there is
one sinful soul for whom to suffer.

Charles Allen Dinsmore, *Atonement in Literature and Life*
(Boston: Mifflin and Co, 1906), p. 232, quoted in D. M. Baillie,
God was in Christ: An Essay on Incarnation and Atonement
(London and Boston: Faber and Faber, 1986), p. 194.

Contents

Part 4 The Cross in the Gospels

Preface

Hanging by a Thread: The Questions of the Cross, which I published in 2016, is a book for sceptics. It addresses what I understand as the key objections to belief in Christ, and seeks to turn each one into a reason for faith. This book takes a different approach.

It starts in its introduction by setting out, as simply as I know how, my understanding of the meaning of Jesus' crucifixion: that's to say, the manifestation of God's utter with in the face of multiple dimensions of without; or the cost and glory of God's will in Christ to be with us whatever the consequences.

After a section that lays out important background territory – of the cross in Jesus' story and of the standard understandings of the cross – I then go on to attempt a biblical theology of the cross. I start with the cross in the Old Testament, engaging with six signal motifs. I don't attempt sustained exegesis: instead I'm trying to identify the power of these motifs today. Thus I illustrate my discussion with examples from literature and film, stirring in the reader a sense that the Old Testament is the gospel – and not just a prologue or prophecy of it.

In Part Three I move on to the New Testament Epistles. Again I'm not looking to offer scriptural commentary. I'm taking six images for the cross found in the epistles and through literary, cinematic and pastoral reflection, sensing the power of these images today.

Finally, in Part Four, I explore perhaps more familiar ground – the gospels. The style remains the same. Sometimes my treatment follows the text closely; more often I am seeking to encompass the emotional and existential range of what the text describes and implies. I have already, in the introduction, set out what I see as the central significance of the cross. But the cross is, in the end, inexhaustible, and if I find fault with conventional theories it's not because they're too outlandish but too narrow. The Bible has no single understanding of the significance of the cross. So I have judged it best to set out my core understanding, and then amplify that understanding with an array of largely but not wholly dovetailing reflections.

The book concludes with materials to assist group or individual study.

I've written the book because I sense that a lot of preachers don't dwell on the cross because they believe it belongs to Good Friday; and then find that a lot of Christians don't come to church on Good Friday. That means a lot of Christians feel unease at the way the cross is spoken of in conventional theories of the atonement – but don't know quite what to put in their place. Which leaves an abiding tentativeness that the cross is central, fundamental ... but we're not quite sure what precisely it actually means – although we're pretty sure it doesn't mean exactly what a lot of people seem so sure it means. In place of that tentativeness I want to put conviction and a sense of new discovery.

Like much of my work this material arose in the context of preaching and of shaping liturgy. I have been blessed to work for the last 15 years with outstanding ministers and musicians and attentive and responsive congregations, at both Duke University Chapel in North Carolina and St Martin-in-the-Fields in London. I'm greatly in their debt. Some of the material in the introduction and in Part Four, chapter six, appeared in a shorter form in my *A Nazareth Manifesto: Being with God* (Oxford: Wiley Blackwell 2015). The story about the firefighter in Part One, chapter five, also appears in my *Face to Face: Meeting Christ in Friend and Stranger* (Norwich: Canterbury 2019).

This is not the last word on the cross. That would be absurd.

It's an invitation to deeper exploration and devotion. In Charles Wesley's words, 'In vain the firstborn seraph tries to sound the depths of love divine. 'Tis mercy all! Let earth adore, let angel minds enquire no more.' But the rest of us will enquire. For a long time yet.

Introduction:
A Cross in the Heart of God

When it was noon, darkness came over the whole land until three in the afternoon. At three o'clock Jesus cried out with a loud voice, 'Eloi, Eloi, lema sabachthani?' which means, 'My God, my God, why have you forsaken me?' When some of the bystanders heard it, they said, 'Listen, he is calling for Elijah.' And someone ran, filled a sponge with sour wine, put it on a stick, and gave it to him to drink, saying, 'Wait, let us see whether Elijah will come to take him down.' Then Jesus gave a loud cry and breathed his last. (Mark 15.33–37)

Hundreds of years ago when I was a bachelor, I was having a drink in a park with a friend and we were locked into what I now look back on as one of our interminable disagreements. There was a band on stage close by and the lead vocalist was finishing her song. She looked hard at the drummer with the unforgettable words, 'No matter what you do-oo, ah only, ah only, ah only, ah only, ah only wanna be with you.' To which the drummer replied, 'Da-nah nah.' My female friend looked at me winsomely and said, 'Do you think they argue as well?' It was a sweet moment. (Although not enough to save the relationship.) But ever since then, this song's been one of my favorites. It wasn't till many years later that I realized it expressed the essence of Good Friday and the heart of the Christian faith.

The Gospel of Matthew begins with the angel's promise that the Messiah will be called Emmanuel – God *with* us. The

Gospel ends with Jesus' promise to his disciples, 'Remember, I am *with* you always, to the end of the age.' In between we get Jesus' promise to the church, 'Where two or three are gathered in my name, I am there *with* them.' The Gospel of Mark says Jesus 'appointed twelve, whom he also named apostles, to be *with* him'. When the scribes and Pharisees criticize Jesus, they say, 'Why does he eat *with* tax collectors and sinners?' And when Jesus gets really fed up with the disciples, he says, 'You faithless generation, how much longer must I be *with* you?' The Gospel of Luke begins with the angel saying to Mary, 'The Lord is *with* you;' when the father of the prodigal son is comforting the elder brother out in the field, he says, 'Son, you are always *with* me, and all that is mine is yours.' On the Emmaus road the disciples say to the risen Jesus, 'Stay *with* us.'

And, perhaps most significantly of all, the Gospel of John begins with the words, 'The Word was *with* God, and the Word was God. He was in the beginning *with* God.' Most famously it goes on to say, 'The Word was made flesh and dwelt *with* us.' Later, Jesus says, 'You always have the poor *with* you.' And on the night before he dies, Jesus says at supper, 'I am not alone because the Father is *with* me.' In other words, if there is one word that sums up all four gospels, that word is '*with*'. Jesus' ministry, above all else, is about being *with* us, in pain and glory, in sorrow and in joy, in quiet and in conflict, in death and in life.

And that same '*with*' is even more evident when we turn to the relationship within the Godhead itself, the Trinity of Father, Son and Holy Spirit. God is three, which means God is a perfect symmetry of *with*, three beings wholly present to one another, without envy, without misunderstanding, without irritation, without selfishness, without two ganging up against the third, without anger, without anxiety, without mistrust. So present to one another, so rapt in love, and cherishing, and mutuality, and devotion, that they seem to transcend *with* and become *in*.

That sense of so relishing and rejoicing in *with* that you long for and aspire to *in* is a yearning human beings know well. It's integral to sexual desire. For many people sexual desire is a longing to translate *with* into *in*, to intensify the joy of being in another's presence into a physical and spiritual experience of mutual indwelling. But sexual desire has complications and limitations. It's full of envy, misunderstanding, anxiety and mistrust. So much sexual expression is a grasping at *in* that's not preceded, surrounded, accompanied and followed by a profound and lasting *with*. Can there possibly be a kind of mutual indwelling that's beyond such human limitations?

The indwelling of the Trinity is exactly that. The Father, the Son and the Holy Spirit are so *with* one another that it seems they are *in* one another. And, to the extent that they are *in* one another, we call God not three, but one. These three are so *with* that they are one, three persons in one substance, always affirming one another's difference and distinctness in person and presence, but always bearing within one another the whole being of the other two persons. The Trinity is the perfect equilibrium of three persons so *with* that they are *in*, but *in* in such a way that they are still *with*.

Given this perfection of being, this intersection of being *with* and being *in*, the astonishing mystery is why the Trinity's life is not simply self-contained, but becomes open to creation, to fragile existence, to life, to human beings. Surely the grasping, mistrustful, anxious and small-minded human spirit would ruin the perfection of the Trinity. Or could it possibly be that God's grace is more infectious than our folly? Could it conceivably be that the mutual indwelling love of the Trinity could outlast and ultimately transform our human fragility and perversity? That's the dynamic behind the whole Bible, the whole of history, the whole gospel. If God's life opens up to us, will it destroy God – or transform us? And if it ultimately transforms *us*, how much will it cost *God*?

This is what it means to say there was a cross in the heart of God from the foundation of the world. Being with us was in the heart of the Trinity from the beginning. Jesus was not a response to the unfortunate event of the Fall. Jesus was the reason for creation. Jesus was always going to experience the full horror of humanity's rejection of God. God's life opening to us was always going to cost God everything. The cross in the heart of God will always be there. The scar remains, however much the resurrection demonstrates that the devastation of the cross does not damage God's will to be with us. The scar will be there forever. It will always show us how much God's identity is immersed in being with us.

At the foot of the cross we see the very heart of God and the very worst in ourselves. When I was 17 I went to hear a well-known evangelist speak at the big theatre in the town where I lived. I knew my sister had heard him, and I remembered she'd said he was quite something. He preached what we might call a Mel Gibson gospel. In other words he gave us the third-degree, gruesome, vivid and unforgettable detail of the cross, in the style of the film *The Passion of the Christ*. In sweaty language and wincing imagery, he described what the process of crucifixion did to the heart, lungs, rib cage, wind–pipe, face, eyes, cheeks, hips, feet and hands. When 45 minutes was up and he'd made our nails curl, our stomachs wail, our throats dry and our eyes weep, he invited us all to come to the front and make a commitment.

I didn't go. The next day I called my sister. She said, 'D'you feel guilty about not going forward?' I said, 'Yes.' She said, 'You shouldn't. You see, it's not the gospel. If you look in the Bible, the gospels tell us almost nothing about the physical details of the crucifixion. Jesus suffered terribly, don't get me wrong, but lots of people suffered then, some even worse than him, and lots of people have suffered since and still do, some of them probably more so than he did. The gospel isn't about some contest of pain in which Jesus came out the winner. The gospel is not that Jesus physically suffered. It's that he was forsaken.'

Forsaken. Jesus' last words, in Mark's gospel, are, 'My God, my God, why have you forsaken me?' At first sight, this is simply the last in a chain of abandonments. The disciples flee,

Peter denies, Judas betrays, now the Father forsakes. It's a litany of desertion. And there's something in this litany. Remember, if the crucial word in the gospel is *with*, then the events leading up to Jesus' crucifixion are a heartless and wholesale dismantling of that *with*. Jesus is left *without* all those he worked so hard to be *with* – the disciples, the authorities, the poor – and all of them have not just disappeared, but actively deserted or betrayed him. Jesus is still *with* us, but we, at this most precious moment of all, are not *with* him.

But these abandonments are nothing compared to the one that really matters. The cross isn't just an extreme version of a generic human experience of being alone and in pain and unjustly punished and cruelly ridiculed. The cross is a unique event. It's not unique because of how much pain Jesus felt or how much love he'd previously expended. It's unique because the Holy Trinity is the utter presence of unalloyed *with* and at the moment of Jesus' death, that *with* is, for a brief moment and for the only instant in eternal history, lost.

We've seen that *with* is the very essence of God's being within the life of the Trinity, and the very essence of God's being towards us in Christ. And yet, at this unique moment, that *with* is obscured. Like the clouds coming across the sun, shrouding the earth in shadow, the essence of God, always three persons in perfect relationship, always God's life shaped to be *with* us – that essence is for a moment lost. This is the most poignant and terrifying moment in all history. The two things we think we can know for certain – that God is a Trinity of persons in perfect and eternal relationship, and that God is always present *with* us in Christ through the Spirit – these two certainties are, for a moment, taken away. The universe's deepest realities have become unhinged. The Son is not *with* the Father, even though he desperately wants to be. The Father is not *with* the Son, breaking our whole notion of their eternal presence one with another. This is the most vivid picture of hell we could imagine: not just our being separated from God; but God being separated from God, God being out of God's own reach.

The cross is Jesus' ultimate demonstration of being *with* us – but in the cruellest irony of all time, it's the instant Jesus finds that neither we, nor the Father, are *with* him. Every aspect of being *not-with*, of being *with-out*, clusters together at this agonizing moment. Jesus experiences the reality of human sin, because sin is fundamentally living *without* God. Jesus experiences the depth of suffering, because suffering is more than anything the condition of being *without* comfort. Jesus experiences the horror of death, because death is the word we give to being *without* all things – without breath, without connectedness, without consciousness, without a body. Jesus experiences the biggest alienation of all, the state of being *without* the Father, and thus being not-God – being, for this moment, without the *with* that is the essence of God.

And Jesus' words at this most terrifying moment are these. 'My God, my God, why have you forsaken me?' He's still talking to the Father, even at the moment of naming that the *with* has gone. He's still talking in intimate terms – calling the Father 'My God.' These words come out of the most profound level of trust, the most fathomless depth of *with* and *in*. It's sometimes pointed out that this is the first line of Psalm 22, and that the psalm as a whole is one of hope. But to suggest that really this cry from the cross is an elaborate word of triumph and trust, and that Jesus' recognition of abandonment is all part of a tidy plan, is simply to shield oneself from the unique horror and wonder of this moment. The most tantalizing thing is that Jesus' last words are a question – a question that doesn't receive an answer. The question should rattle us to our bones.

The question shows us that Jesus has given everything that he is for the cause of being *with* us, for the cause of embracing us within the essence of God's being. He's given so much – even despite our determination to be *without* him. And yet he's given beyond our imagination, because for the sake of our being *with* the Father he has, for this moment, lost his own being *with* the Father. And the Father has longed so much to be *with* us that he has, for this moment, lost his being *with* the Son, which is the essence of his being.

These two astonishing discoveries, the Father's losing the Son for us, and the Son's losing the Father for us, rattle our bones because they make us wonder 'Is all then lost?' – not just for us, but even for God. Has the Trinity lost its identity for nothing? If we don't experience a shiver of this greatest of all horrors at this moment, then we haven't allowed ourselves truly to enter Good Friday. But this deepest of fears is what will find an answer in two days' time, when we find that neither sin, nor suffering, nor death, nor alienation has the last word. *With* is restored at Easter and, on the day of Ascension, *with* has the last word.

Is our alienation from God really so profound that it pushes God to such lengths to reverse and heal it? We don't want to believe it. But here it is, in front of our eyes. That's what the cross is – our cowardice and cruelty confronted by God's wondrous love. Is being *with* us forever really worth God going to such lengths to secure? Now that is, perhaps, the most awesome question of all. It takes us to the heart of God's identity and the heart of our own. Can we really believe God thought we were worth it? Are our paltry lives worth the Trinity setting aside the essence of its identity in order that we might be *with* God and incorporated into God's life forever?

At the central moment in history, Jesus, the incarnate Son of God, has to choose between being with the Father or being with us. And he chooses us. At the same time the Father has to choose between letting the Son be with us or keeping the Son to himself. And he chooses to let the Son be with us. That's the choice on which our eternal destiny depends. That's the epicentre of the Christian faith. That's our very definition of love.

We hear the simple words of the Holy Trinity, singing to us more passionately, fondly and sacrificially than we can ever have known: 'Ah only, ah only, ah only, ah only, ah only wanna be with you ...' This book is a series of reflections that invite us to answer one question: What are we singing back?

PART I

The Cross and the Passion of Christ

The key word in this section is context. Having, in the introduction, set out how I understand the cross as the demonstration of the centrality, cost and promise of God being with us, I need now to pause and take account of two dimensions in which this assertion is heard. My argument in this section is that the cross is invariably separated from its political and social context. By setting out that context in some detail and by briefly addressing the conventional ways of talking about the cross, I aim to show why a reassessment of the cross is timely and necessary. The rest of the book amplifies and exemplifies the claims made in this section.

I

The Main Characters

Towards the end their stories, the gospels assemble on stage all the key actors in the drama. Here are the Romans, the ones with the ability to force the issue through military power. Here are the Jerusalem authorities, the Jewish leaders who'd decided that collaboration with the Romans was the only way to survive in a period of foreign occupation. Here are the rebels, Barabbas and the two prisoners with whom Jesus is crucified, who have set their hearts on clearing out the Romans and don't have much time for the Jerusalem authorities either.

These three groups are the main players. And then, in the background, are the two groups with whom the reader is meant to identify. On the one hand is the crowd, the host of people who project onto Jesus their own hopes for national restoration or personal healing, and swing from adulation on Palm Sunday to baying for blood on Good Friday. On the other hand are the disciples, full of promises of undying loyalty and plenty close enough to see exactly who Jesus is, but nonetheless unravelling in a spiral of stumbling timidity and outright betrayal.

The gospels don't give us systematic theology or social ethics in propositional form. They give us a story. But that story gives us all we need to know about who Jesus is and what he requires of us. We can see this if we contrast Jesus with the three main players in the Holy Week drama – the Romans, the authorities and the rebels.

Let's start with the Romans. Every time a Roman general had a successful campaign, he would march on his horse in a triumphant procession into Rome. On Palm Sunday, Jesus marches into Jerusalem on a colt. This is a spoof. Jesus is sitting on a donkey, not a horse: an agricultural tool, not a weapon of war; a tractor, not a tank. It's hard to see how the Roman governor would have missed a joke directed at him. Jesus is coming to receive what is rightfully his, yet he is doing so not with armies of soldiers, but surrounded by people coming in from the fields, country people, exactly the people most oppressed by the regime. Jesus' triumphal entry ends not at the Roman palace but at the Temple. It's pretty clear where he thinks real power lies in Israel. Later, Jesus is asked a question about paying taxes to Caesar. This is forcing him to make a direct choice between the Jerusalem authorities, who went along with Roman domination, and the rebels, who regarded taxes as blasphemy. Jesus' deeply ironic response – 'give God what is God's' – points to the fact that everything the Romans think they control in fact lies in God's power. Later again, when Pilate asks, 'Are you the King of the Jews?', Jesus doesn't deny it. It's not surprising Pilate has Jesus executed. These three episodes show that Jesus is claiming an authority way beyond that which Pilate has, and that deep down, he doesn't take Pilate terribly seriously.

Let's now look at the Jerusalem leaders. In theory, they were longing for a Messiah to remove the Romans, restore and unite Israel, and inaugurate an unprecedented era of peace. But a bit of historical perspective might be helpful here. There was already a family that regarded themselves as the house of the kings in Israel, and that was the half-Jewish house of Herod. Herod the Great tried to polish off Jesus at birth, and Herod Antipas was now around, eager to finish the job. Herod's family had brought in the family of Caiaphas from overseas to serve as High Priests. So the High Priest was in the pocket of the puppet king, who was under the thumb of the Roman governor. And all these people garnered large sums of money through extorting tax from the country people. This was not a democracy, and the gospels assume that those Jews who exercised power did so by sucking up to the Romans and oppressing their own people. By riding into Jerusalem on

Palm Sunday, Jesus is saying he is the real leader of Israel. By questioning the status of the Temple, Jesus is saying he is the true intermediary between God and the people. By debating with each rival group in the Temple precincts as the week goes on, Jesus is saying he has more wisdom than the scribes, more holiness than the Pharisees, more authority than the Sadducees and more power than the Herodians. When brought before the Sanhedrin, Jesus says, 'You will see the Son of Man seated at the right hand of the Power' – in other words, if you think you're judging me, the joke's on you.

So then to the rebels. Once Jesus has dismissed the option of living in Rome's pocket, it might seem that armed rebellion was the only alternative left to him. Perhaps the most plausible explanation for Judas' betrayal of Jesus is that Judas assumed Jesus would overturn his own arrest and launch the violent overthrow of Roman rule for which so many longed. So Judas must have found Palm Sunday a bewildering experience: Jesus has the world shouting for him, but does nothing. And even the cleansing of the Temple is a curious kind of revolution: the aggression is directed toward sheep, cattle, coins, tables and doves. No one's hurt, let alone killed. It is a vivid symbolic gesture, not an element of a violent insurrection. When it comes to the arrest in Gethsemane, Jesus says, 'Have you come out with swords and clubs to arrest me as though I were a terrorist?' The scene in Gethsemane makes two things clear. One is that Jesus had established a new form of life that others saw as a political threat. The other is that Jesus had no intention of translating that social programme into a violent revolution.

Any Christian who has lived through 9/11, the invasions of Afghanistan and Iraq, the 7/7 bombings and the tyranny of Islamic State could have come to the conclusion that the story that mattered was really all about the government, the religious leaders and the terrorists. These seem to be the people who set the agenda. But the passiontide story suggests that Jesus doesn't concentrate on the Romans, the Jerusalem authorities and the rebels. These, in different ways, are the people who put

Jesus to death. But they aren't the people the story is about. The story is about the other two groups.

The other two groups are the disciples and the crowd. Like everyone else, neither the disciples nor the crowd come out of the story particularly well. But they portray the two key dimensions of what Jesus is doing in his passion. The crowd represents what we might call the 'public' aspect of Jesus' passion. Jesus dies for a whole bunch of people, some who acknowledge him, some who love him, some who misunderstand him, some who are unaware of him, some who hate him. He dies, in short, for 'the whole world'. The whole world doesn't put him to death, but the whole world exhibits the kinds of jealousy, mob spirit, cynicism, fear and sheer perversity that did put him to death. Meanwhile the disciples represent what we might call the 'personal' aspect of Jesus' passion. The death of Jesus is indeed an event in time that brings about the transformation of the whole world. But it's portrayed in the context of an intense story of intimacy and betrayal. It's in the intimacy of the Last Supper, as bread is being dipped in the bowl, that Judas slips out to betray Jesus. It's in the intimacy of the garden, as Jesus holds fast to his Father, that those he has called his friends disintegrate around him. Passiontide is a story not so much about conventional notions of power such as military dictatorship, religious authority or terrorist violence, but about a power that's at the same time far greater and more intimate than any of them – God's enduring love for the whole world, and God's intense love for us, Christ's intimate friends.

So as we look at the meaning of the cross, we begin to make the transition from the politics, betrayal and terror of the characters around Jesus to the very pressing and sometimes similar issues of our own lives as Christians. And the questions for us as we approach the cross are these three. Number one, Do I assume politics is all about the government, religion all about the professional religious, and power all about the terrorists? Or do I look where Jesus looked, to the breadth of the endlessly diverse crowd and the depth of intimate discipleship?

Number two, Do I realize Jesus' passion is about the whole world, that these days transformed the nature and destiny of the whole world, not just showing us the full horror of human sin but opening out the full possibility of the redemption of all things? Number three, Do I realize that Jesus' passion is also about me?

To examine the cross is to step out of our assumptions about power – the power that lives in the hands of the government, in the hearts of religious leaders, or in the minds of the terrorists. It's to gather around the true power in the universe, made present in the fragile form of Jesus Christ – a power that transforms the whole world, and can even transform us.

2

The Standard Approaches

How does Jesus save us? As we explore our understanding of the cross we might do well to set out the historic and widely held answers to that question better to appreciate what our answer to the question might be today.

The first answer to the question focuses on Jesus' *birth*. The key date is Christmas Day. It says that Jesus saves us by re-enacting or 'recapitulating' every aspect of our human existence, setting right what was out of joint. Thus Adam disobeyed God by eating from the tree, whereas Christ obeyed God by dying on the tree. Christ sanctifies every dimension of human life. We are saved because in Christ the corruptible, finite quality of human nature is joined to the immortal, incorruptible character of God and thus transformed. The crucifixion and resurrection show that Christ also transforms death; but the real moment of salvation is the incarnation itself.

The second answer focuses on Jesus' *life*. This is sometimes called the moral theory. It suggests that we human beings are the audience for Jesus. In his kindness and generosity, in his ministry to outcasts, sinners and the sick, in his close relationship to the Father, in his prophetic confrontation with those who kept people under oppression, and most of all in his selfless and faithful journey to the cross, Jesus offers himself as the one who transforms our hearts to follow in his steps in the way of sacrificial love. Think of the words, 'my richest gain I count but loss and pour contempt on all my pride'. This theory is sometimes described as subjective, because Jesus doesn't seem objectively to change anything about fundamental reality – it is we who are changed. The danger can be that Jesus simply illustrates what we already knew by methods other than revelation.

The third answer focuses on the suffering laid on Jesus as he went to and hung on the cross. Here the crucial moment is Good Friday. The theory is that humanity had accumulated an unpayable level of guilt before God. Humanity therefore deserved eternal punishment. But through a unique act of grace, God sent Jesus to face this punishment in our place. This is often called penal substitution. The words of Isaiah 53 are very significant and echo through Christian history: 'surely he has borne our griefs and carried our sorrows ... he was wounded for our transgressions, he was bruised for our iniquities ... the Lord has laid on him the iniquity of us all.' It's important to note here that what's most important is that Jesus *suffered*. While his death is significant and the resurrection is not ignored, the theory rests so much on the necessity of punishment that attention often focuses chiefly on the extent of Jesus' sufferings. Our imaginations focus on how much suffering it would take to substitute for the sins of the whole world. A characteristically Protestant version of this theory is that Jesus suffered not so much for humanity's sins in general but for each individual's sins in particular. Such an objective view of salvation leaves an open question over whether one is automatically saved whether one believes or not.

The fourth answer also concentrates on Good Friday but this time focuses on Jesus' *death*. Jesus is a sacrifice that sets right our relationship to God. In this view the problem is one of debt. The most influential view says that the debt is to God's honour. The failure of humanity to do justice before God creates a terrible imbalance in the moral universe. Only humanity must pay the debt but only God can pay the debt. Hence the God-human, Jesus. When Jesus dies he repays the debt of honour with interest, and it is this interest, known as merit, that humanity can access through the sacraments and thus find salvation. This is a characteristically Roman Catholic view. An older version of this theory also focused on Jesus' actual death but saw the debt as owed not to God but to Satan. In this view Adam and Eve had sold humanity to the Devil and thus God needed to ransom humanity the way one would redeem a slave. However, Jesus' death, while succeeding as a ransom and buying us back, was in fact a trick because Jesus rose from death and escaped the Devil's clutches. Whenever we use the word redemption we hint at this ransom theory, but the theory has in fact been out of fashion for a millennium or so.

The fifth answer focuses on Jesus' resurrection. If substitution sees salvation as decided in a law court, then this fifth view sees it as a battle. Death cannot hold Jesus; he destroys death and opens out the prospect of eternal life by rising from the grave. The resurrection of Jesus brings about our resurrection by dismantling the hold of death not just once but for all time. Again there's a significant ambiguity here about whether this resurrection model logically means automatic salvation for all. Either way, the key word is victory. This is the characteristic Eastern Orthodox view. It has achieved a revival in the West particularly among those keen to stress how Jesus' resurrection doesn't just save the individual soul but transforms whole societies by dismantling all the social, economic and cultural forces that oppress people.

Looking at the five theories, I'm sure many readers will have been encouraged at some stage in their life to regard only one of them as the whole story and to distrust or disapprove of the others. But I imagine a similar number would like to take the best bits of all of them and simply say, if there's salvation coming from Christ, bring it on, I'll have as much as is going, please. It's important to say that there are scriptural texts that lend support to all five views, so anyone who is in the habit of promoting suspicion around any of them will have the relevant scriptural texts to deal with.

But I want to suggest that there's a real danger with all five theories. And that is that they're theories. That's to say, they're disembodied constructs that pay little or no attention to the context and contours of Jesus' life. The single word that epitomizes the context and contours of Jesus' life is Israel. Most of the theories of the way Jesus saves us exclude almost all the circumstantial detail that makes up the gospels. There's a good reason for that: these theories set forth ways in which any individual anywhere can find salvation in Christ. But the trouble is, the circumstantial detail is the gospel.

Let me explain. When you hear all these theories together, you get a picture of an agitated God, worried about a code of honour or searching around to find some booty to pay off Satan, subject to some eternal law court that says what God can and can't do, or fixing a heavenly imbalance as if it were a leaky roof. You see a picture of the Holy Trinity either subject to some eternal rule of engagement that's not of their own making, or gathered together in the board room scratching their heads over Adam's fall as if it were a hole in the budget. What's this got to do with the Jesus of the gospels? Almost nothing.

Instead, the Jesus of the gospels reenacts the story of Israel, going down into Egypt with Joseph like Israel did, beginning at the Jordan like Israel did, facing 40 days in the wilderness like Israel faced 40 years, calling 12 disciples like Israel had 12 tribes and most of all assembling around himself and transforming those facing internal exile in Israel, the leper, the prostitute, the tax collector, the social outcast, just as he came to transform the internal exile of Israel which found itself under Roman occupation. Five hundred years before Christ, Israel had returned from exile not knowing whether it had learned its lessons about sin, redemption and the character of God from its time in Babylon or not. Finding itself in Jesus' time living under internal exile, it seemed not. Jesus emerged from Galilee with resonances of every major player in Israel's history. He was the second Adam; he was the one righteous man like Noah; he made a new people like Abraham; he was the new Israel like Jacob; he went down to despair and rose up to save his people like Joseph; he led his people to liberation like Moses; he was the ultimate king like David; he was a healer and troublemaker like Elijah; he spoke truth in the face of alien power like Daniel; he put his life on the line to save his people like Esther.

By facing the way of the cross Jesus took the story of Israel on himself and went into internal exile among his own people. Exile names the unique condition in which Israel discovered that God brings liberation through suffering and that God is made known through and to Gentiles as well as Jews. But what is most crucial about exile is that in exile Israel saw a new face of God. Israel found it was closer to God in exile than it had ever been in the Promised Land. What Israel found was the God of with. Before exile God had primarily been seen as for – a God who kept one side of the covenant, to bless Israel with prosperity, population and pride so long as Israel responded with worship and obedience. But in exile Israel discovered a God who was with them in their plight and shared with them in their sorrows. In exile Israel wrote down its story and perceived how God had been with them always. Because Israel had met the God of with in the face of suffering and grief, the early church could discern that God had never more been with them than in the suffering of grief of the cross. The cross demonstrated utterly what had first been perceived in exile – that God is made known in the face of disadvantage and despair like never before.

The cross was not, I believe, inevitable. It might not have been like this. The cross was always likely, even probable, because this is what happens when the utter goodness of God is utterly vulnerable in the presence of the short-sightedness and cruelty of human beings. Hence Jesus predicted it three times. But I don't believe the cross was inevitable. Israel could have said yes. I can imagine that if Israel had rallied behind Jesus the nation might have experienced much of what Jesus called the kingdom of God. What a threat to Rome that would have been – not a threat of arms, but a threat of a changed society. Israel might then have been subject to a collective cross at the hands of the Romans as transforming as the cross of the individual man Christ. Isaiah 53, the story of the suffering servant, would have applied to the whole nation after all. But by rejecting Jesus – and by telling us that Jesus died practically alone, the gospels make clear this was utter rejection – his people put God to the ultimate test. And most wonderfully of all, God turned that rejection into the ultimate demonstration of grace, at Easter turning brutal death into breathtaking glory, and at Pentecost, in the birth of the church and its clothing in the Holy Spirit, making available to the whole world the homecoming brought about through Christ.

This is, I believe, how God meets us in the crucified Jesus. Not through a decontextualized theory that posits a faraway God doing curious deals in the light of arbitrary codes of debt, justice or honour: but through the Jews, God's everlasting love for them and through them for all the nations and the whole creation; and through the discovery of a God of with so much deeper and more profound than a God of for. The church is that body of people who declare they want to be in continuity with this story, who in baptism accept that this story is their story, who know themselves to be in exile from God and see Jesus as the one who went into exile for them and with whom they can identify when they are in exile too. The church is not a collection of individuals who make their own private arrangements about which theory of salvation they fancy and join up with a bunch of others who favour the same one. It is those people who believe they are called to be the context of Jesus' story.

The church is called to demonstrate that salvation in Christ isn't just a theory. If we start with one or more of the five theories of how Jesus saves us, we'll be casting around for a church that gets our favourite theory right. But it should be the other way round. We should seek to embody in our church life such hopefulness, such faithfulness, such patience, such endurance, such forgiveness, such truthfulness that could only be possible if Jesus is with us, whatever, however, forever. We should be a context that demands an explanation, a living mystery that invites scrutiny. We should be a people coming out of exile, out of the exile of sin, of oppression, of estrangement, of fear, of suffering, of death. We should be a people helping to bring others out of exile, of despair, of loneliness, of regret, of humiliation. We should be a people who speak of the God who was made known to us in exile, the God who went into exile for us, and the God who is with us in our exile. We should be a context that demands an explanation. The explanation is Jesus.

In the gospels the context of Jesus' story is the disciples, the poor and the authorities, who together make up Israel. For much of the last 2000 years, Jesus' identity and story has been presented as if it needed no context and thus the church has been invisible. But today, it is we who are called to be the context of Jesus' story. We are some kind of mixture of the disciples, the poor and the authorities. We must ensure that salvation in Christ is never just a theory. It's a reality. It has to be seen in context. And it could just be that that context, at the moment, doesn't just mean the Jews. It means us.

PART 2

The Cross in the Old Testament

3

Covenant

I believe that the longing to be with us in Jesus was the reason God created the world. But this longing was always going to carry immense risk, and that the fundamental choice God made was to say, 'I am going to carry the consequences of that risk and I am not going to expect humanity to shoulder a burden it cannot bear.' In other words, however much we have refused God's invitation to be with us it has always remained an invitation and not an imposition, and the cost of restoration and reconciliation is something that God has borne, not us. Since that has been so from the very beginning I believe it's appropriate to say that there has been a cross in the heart of God since the foundation of the world, and there will be forever, even after the last tear has been wiped away from the last eye. The cross was one event at one particular time; but it demonstrated what has always been true, that God will never give up on us, however much we may fail to desire or deserve it. And because it has always been so, I want in this section to explore what we might call the cross in the Old Testament. I'm not talking about prophecies, but about ways in which the Old Testament shows us the meaning and character of the cross. The place to begin is with Noah.

> The Lord saw that the wickedness of humankind was great in the earth, and that every inclination of the thoughts of their hearts was only evil continually. And the Lord was sorry that he had made humankind on the earth, and it grieved him to his heart. So the Lord said, 'I will blot out from the earth the

human beings I have created – people together with animals and creeping things and birds of the air, for I am sorry that I have made them.' But Noah found favour in the sight of the Lord.

In the six hundred and first year, the waters were dried up from the earth. Then God said to Noah, 'Go out of the ark. Bring out with you every living thing that is with you of all flesh – birds and animals and every creeping thing that creeps on the earth – so that they may abound on the earth, and be fruitful and multiply on the earth.'

The Lord said in his heart, 'I will never again curse the ground because of humankind. Then God said to Noah, 'I establish my covenant with you, that never again shall all flesh be cut off by the waters of a flood. This is the sign of the covenant: I have set my bow in the clouds, for the inclination of the human heart is evil from youth; nor will I ever again destroy every living creature as I have done.' (Genesis 6–9, abridged)

The thing we fear above anything else is destruction. If we can get our heads round it, we fear the Big Crunch, the opposite of the Big Bang, through which one day the centrifugal expansion of the universe will cease and a centripetal implosion of the universe will begin and all will be sucked back into the vortex and disappear. More tangibly we fear a giant meteor that could obliterate the earth at one go. More urgently we fear climate change could alter the ecology of the planet and make life unsustainable, we fear a nuclear war in which two or more deranged world leaders provoke global megadeath. But each of these nightmares is but a larger version of our daily harrowing anticipation of our own destruction in death.

The story of Noah is about destruction. The rain fell for 40 days and the waters swelled for 150 days. God 'blotted out every living thing that was on the face of the ground, human beings and animals and creeping things and birds of the air'. We're given a reason for this destruction: 'The Lord saw that the wickedness of humankind was great in the earth, and that every inclination of the thoughts of their hearts was only evil continually.' So it sounds like this is simply a case of judgement: God made the world good, it turned out evil, so God destroyed it. End of.

But it turns out there's more to it than that. The real drama of the Noah story doesn't lie in the flood, the ark, the animals, the two-by-two, the raven and the dove. The real drama lies in the heart of God. Here is a parent with a wayward child. We all know the heavy thud of the words, 'I'm not angry – I'm disappointed.' The Lord, we're told, was very sorry, and was grieved. Or, in our language, was devastated. Think about that word for a moment: this is a story about devastation; initially devastation wrought upon the earth – but more profoundly, devastation wrought upon God's heart. This is a story about a face-off between the human heart (corrupt, complicit, carnal) and God's heart (wretched, dejected, sad). God's power is quickly displayed, but God's love ultimately prevails.

Out of this story emerges a series of crucial details that characterize the whole of the Bible and continue to shape our faith today. There's no question that creation in general and humanity in particular, though God-breathed and beautiful, is nonetheless flawed, fragile and often feckless. There's no naïveté or wishful thinking in this story. But see what surfaces nonetheless. God says, 'I'm going to be with you anyway.' God makes a covenant with a people that have shown themselves to be unworthy and ungrateful. The whole of creation depended on God's desire to be with us; but the astonishing thing is that God continues to desire to be with us even when in innumerable ways we've shown little or no desire to reciprocate.

To confirm this amazing desire, God makes a covenant. And what does that covenant say? 'I will never again destroy every living creature as I have done.' That's a huge promise. Never say never. But God does say never. Destruction is ruled out as a tactic, however bad humanity gets. That means God has to find another way. And this is the dynamic that unlocks the whole

Bible. Destruction isn't an option. Israel and God are sealed into a relationship where termination isn't available. They have to find a way to be with one another. Will God regret that promise? We shall see. To demonstrate what it means, God sets a bow in the clouds. We know what that bow is: no children's Noah's Ark set is complete without a rainbow. But a bow is no idle thing: it's not something with which you play a cello. It's a weapon of war: a bow that accompanies an arrow. God has put that weapon away, in heaven. God's sword and shield have been laid down; God ain't going to study war, or floods, or destruction any more. Every time we see a rainbow we're looking at God's promise never to destroy us again. We won't be devastated: but God will.

And out of this intense and dramatic face-off between the corrupt heart of humankind and the grieving heart of God comes a new humanity. Noah, a person who truly walks with God, who walks through the water of death and destruction and enters the new covenant of life and preservation. Noah, who finds God's favour, and from whom comes a new strand of human possibility, which we might even call resurrection.

All these dimensions arise from the Noah story. And that's why this story is the place to begin our understanding of what's taking place between God, humanity and creation as Christ hangs on the cross. Because every single one of these dimensions of Noah are present in Christ. Christ *is* God being with us even when we turn out to be the worst that bad can be. In his passion we see a catalogue of duplicity, denial, betrayal, conspiracy and destruction as grotesque as anything that could have evoked God's disappointment in the days of the ark. Christ *is* the embodiment and renewal of the covenant God first made with Noah. Christ *is* the logical and perhaps inevitable result of God giving up on any idea of destroying the wayward creation – after a whole Old Testament of to-ing and fro-ing between God and Israel, finally there arises one who is utterly Israel and utterly God, who experiences in his own person the destruction God has promised never again to wreak on the earth and who offers in his body the new covenant God makes with humankind. Christ *is* the rainbow in the clouds, the result of God abjuring the weapons of war – and just as when we see the rainbow we recall God's promise, so when we see the cross we behold the fulfilment of that promise at no cost to us and maximum cost to God. And Christ *is* the new humanity that comes on the other side of the flood, for in his resurrection he becomes the firstborn of all creation, the new human being in whom through baptism all people can find life and after whose death there will never again be any cause to doubt God's faithfulness or favour.

Above all, Christ on the cross shows us that, for all our anxiety about the destruction of creation and our own death, the real drama of the story takes place in the heart of God. How *can* God let this happen? How *can* God emerge without breaking a promise not to end the story because it's turning out so badly? How *can* God suffer so terribly? How *can* God love us so much and forgive us so deeply and be faithful to us so enduringly that Christ can hang there with such grief and sadness and pain?

Fifty miles north of Berlin lies the site of the Ravensbrück concentration camp, where 130,000 women were interned during the Holocaust, of whom 50,000 died. When the camp was liberated, a piece of wrapping paper was found near the body of a dead child. On that wrapping paper was the following prayer:

O Lord, remember not only the men and women of good will but also those of evil will. But do not remember all the suffering they have inflicted upon us; remember the fruits we have borne thanks to this suffering – our comradeship, our loyalty, our humility, our courage, our generosity, the greatness of heart which has grown out of all this; and when they come to the judgement, let all the fruits that we have borne be their forgiveness. Amen.

Without context, this prayer makes no sense at all. But to know that this was written on a piece of wrapping paper found near the body of a dead child during the Holocaust makes these some of the greatest words ever prayed. May we find consolation in this – that men and women are capable of much love amidst much hate; that men and women are capable of much mercy and forgiveness amidst an ocean of cynicism and doubt.

The Holocaust was the greatest self-inflicted flood the world has seen since the ark. Here was a tide of destruction to exceed any tsunami of evil. And yet here in the midst of it was one tiny Noah, one person of extraordinary dignity and grace, determined to put her bow in the heavens and repay evil with good. Here was a person who suffered in her own body the destruction inflicted on her whole world. Here was a person who somehow discovered God was with her even though all around her were wondering where God was to be found. Here was a woman who truly said, never again, and showed a way to turn hatred into mercy and cruelty into beauty. Here was Jesus, on the cross in twentieth-century Germany. Here was the heart of God, not hidden, irrelevant and far away, but present, broken and bleeding. Here was the story of Noah, indeed the whole Bible, in one woman. What wondrous love is this, oh my soul, oh my soul. What wondrous love is this, oh my soul.

4

Test

What does it mean for God to provide? The Old Testament is all about God providing. God provides creation and human life in Adam and Eve, new life for Noah after the flood, food amid famine under Joseph, a parting of the Red Sea through Moses, manna in the wilderness, the Law on Sinai, and a new king, Cyrus, who finally sent the Jews home from Babylon to rebuild Jerusalem. The ram in the Abraham and Isaac story stands in for all these signal moments of God's provision.

For the early church, there's one word for what God provides: Jesus. Through Jesus God provides teaching, healing, food, example, prophecy, hope. Most of all, Jesus provides his own body to be the ram that saves all of our bodies. Jesus is the embodiment of God's saving provision: the reason why we trust God.

God tested Abraham. He said to him, 'Abraham!' And he said, 'Here I am.' He said, 'Take your son, your only son Isaac, whom you love, and go to the land of Moriah, and offer him there as a burnt-offering on one of the mountains that I shall show you.' So Abraham rose early in the morning, saddled his donkey, and took two of his young men with him, and his son Isaac; he cut the wood for the burnt-offering, and set out and went to the place in the distance that God had shown him. On the third day Abraham looked up and saw the place far away. Then Abraham said to his young men, 'Stay here with the donkey; the boy and I will go over there; we will worship, and then we will come back to you.'

Abraham took the wood of the burnt-offering and laid it on his son Isaac, and he himself carried the fire and the knife. So the two of them walked on together.

Isaac said to his father Abraham, 'Father!' And he said, 'Here I am, my son.' He said, 'The fire and the wood are here, but where is the lamb for a burnt-offering?' Abraham said, 'God himself will provide the lamb for a burnt-offering, my son.' So the two of them walked on together. When they came to the place that God had shown him, Abraham built an altar there and laid the wood in order. He bound his son Isaac, and laid him on the altar, on top of the wood. Then Abraham reached out his hand and took the knife to kill his son.

But the angel of the Lord called to him from heaven, and said, 'Abraham, Abraham!' And he said, 'Here I am.' He said, 'Do not lay your hand on the boy or do anything to him; for now I know that you fear God, since you have not withheld your son, your only son, from me.' And Abraham looked up and saw a ram, caught in a thicket by its horns. Abraham went and took the ram and offered it up as a burnt-offering instead of his son. So Abraham called that place 'The Lord will provide'; as it is said to this day, 'On the mount of the Lord it shall be provided.' (Genesis 22.1–14)

The story of Abraham and Isaac is an interweaving of two kinds of horror. One is very personal. Abraham carries the fire and the knife. Isaac his son carries the wood for the burnt offering. They walked together for a long time. I wonder what they spoke about. I wonder what Abraham said to Sarah before he set out. And I wonder what he was planning on saying when he returned home alone. Abraham built an altar and laid the wood. He bound his son Isaac and laid him on the altar, on top of the wood. I wonder whether he had to use force. I wonder whether Isaac meekly accepted his fate. Abraham reached out his hand and took the knife to kill his son. I wonder at what point Isaac realized what was about to happen, and what he thought of his father then. That's the first horror. This is about killing your child with fire and knife. The second level of horror is this. Genesis 12 is the beginning of a story. God calls Abraham, Abraham responds. This is going to be a great nation. There's one small problem: Abraham has no descendants. So God provides: old Sarah laughs, but Abraham names the child Isaac, 'he laughs'. On this child lies the destiny of the world. This child is the bearer of the promise. And now God says, 'Take your son, your only son, whom you love, and offer him as a burnt-offering.' No one's laughing now. The story's over almost as soon as it's begun. 'Your only son': there's no future if Abraham does what God commands. This is the second horror: God's story with Israel has come to an end before it's hardly begun.

In the summer of 2015 at the age of 35 my friend and former colleague Kate was told she had stage four colon cancer.[1] All she could think of to say was, 'But I have a son.' Her friends, family and complete strangers all crowded in with counsel. She divided them into three kinds: minimizers, teachers and solvers. Minimizers insist it's not so bad. Kate's sister was on a plane and told her seatmate about the diagnosis. 'Then, as [Kate's sister] wondered when she had signed up to be a contestant in the calamity Olympics, the stranger explained that [Kate's] cancer was vastly preferable to life during the Iranian revolution.' Teachers 'focus on how this experience is supposed to be an education'. One even wished it would be for her a 'Job experience' – as if she needs any further suffering than she already has. Solvers are disappointed that she's not saving herself. As Kate puts it, 'There's always a nutritional supplement, Bible verse or mental process I have not adequately tried. 'Keep smiling! Your attitude determines your destiny!' said a stranger ... in an email, having heard my news somewhere, and I was immediately worn out by the tyranny of prescriptive joy.'

---

1 www.nytimes.com/2018/01/26/opinion/sunday/cancer-what-to-say.html.

Minimizers, teachers and solvers can quickly get to work on the Abraham and Isaac story. But it's no good. The twin horrors of the story remain.

I want to look for a moment more closely at the structure of the story for a clue to what's really at the heart of it, even deeper than layers of horror. The story hangs on three key moments that each have the same shape (and are arranged in three paragraphs above). At the start God calls, 'Abraham.' Abraham responds, 'Here I am.' God commands: 'Take.' At the end the angel calls, 'Abraham.' Abraham responds, 'Here I am.' The angel relaxes the command: 'Do not lay your hand.' In between Isaac calls, 'Father.' Abraham responds in the exact same words, 'Here I am.' Isaac asks, 'Where is the lamb?' But this time, at the centre of the story, Abraham breaks the pattern of the other two interchanges, and answers the question: 'God will provide.'[2]

God will provide. These are the central words in the story. But at the point they are uttered, they seem like they flatly contradict all evidence. Are Abraham's words the statement of the greatest duplicity and cowardice, the refusal to tell Isaac the truth until the very last moment? Or are they the words of the greatest faith, that, even seconds before the terrible sacrifice, Abraham still believed God would find an alternative outcome? The story doesn't tell us.

The story sets in motion two strands in the Old Testament narrative. One is the theme of the lamb. The lamb represents God's mercy. On the night before Israel escapes from slavery in Egypt, the blood of the lamb is smeared on the doorposts so the angel of the Lord knows to pass over the Israelites when it smites the Egyptians. The other is the theme of the son. Israel is God's son, God's only son, the bearer of God's blessing to the world from generation to generation. In the story of Abraham and Isaac, God's mercy in the form of the lamb intervenes to preserve God's blessing in the form of the son.

---

2 Walter Brueggemann, *Genesis: A Bible Commentary for Teaching and Preaching*, John Knox, 1982, pp. 186–7.

But in Jesus the story retains the same shape yet has a different outcome. Again it is set over three days. Again we have a son carrying the wood of sacrifice to a hill of execution. Again we have a son humbly proceeding in the face of horror while only partly comprehending what the father truly has in mind. But this time the lamb of mercy and the son of blessing converge into one. The words 'God will provide' have a very different resonance.

But see how the story of Mount Calvary both repeats and develops the story of Mount Moriah. In the Mount Moriah story, God discovers something God didn't already know: that Abraham, and therefore Israel, will, at the moment of truth, suspend all its doubt, rationality, independence, and dearly held commitments, and place its destiny entirely in God's hands. When Jesus says in Gethsemane, 'Yet not what I will, but what you will', this story is being repeated: Jesus, and therefore Israel, does, at the moment of truth, suspend all its doubt, rationality, independence, and dearly held commitments, and place its destiny entirely in God's hands. But that's not the whole of what's going on at Mount Calvary. There's something more. Humanity discovers something it didn't already know about God: that at the moment of truth, God's sovereignty, dignity, majesty and power will be suspended and God's life will be placed entirely in human hands. If Mount Moriah is where God tested humanity, Mount Calvary is where humanity tested God. And on Mount Calvary we see God's true colours. God provided: and what did God provide? A lamb, yes, a son, yes. But in the end, God provided God.

After Mount Moriah, God knew humanity would in the end be faithful, whatever it cost. After Mount Calvary, humanity knew God would be faithful, whatever it cost. Jesus said, 'Those who want to save their life will lose it, and those who lose their life for my sake will find it.' In Abraham and Jesus, humanity loses its life and finds it. In Jesus, the Holy Trinity loses its life for our sake and finds it.

But why is it necessary to go to such excruciating lengths

to prove such things? Why is it essential so drastically to put one another to the test? What I believe happens on Mount Moriah is that God seeks to find out why Abraham has trusted and obeyed. God is saying, 'Did you respond because of the promise of your descendants becoming a great nation? Did you follow because you wanted security and success and sons and celebrity? In other words, am I in the end a vehicle for you, a means to an end, a ladder you can kick away when I've provided the things you can't get for yourself? Or will you be true to me even if all these things are snatched away?' By putting Isaac in jeopardy, God threatens to take away every promise made to Abraham. Abraham has to choose between life, love, longevity, lineage, land and God. And Abraham chooses God.

In Jesus God is asking the same question but in an even more cosmic way. 'Are you following me because I offer you forgiveness for your past and freedom for your future? Are you believing because faith gives you confidence, reassurance, inspiration, companionship, wisdom and insight? Or will you be true to me even if I am hungry, naked, despised, powerless, cursed, alone?' But in Jesus the same question is turned around and directed to God. 'Will you be with humanity if it is faithful, obedient, devoted, pious and adoring? Or will you be with humanity even if it denies, betrays, flees, despises, executes, derides and tortures? Jesus is us choosing between God's benefits and God, and choosing God. Jesus is also God choosing between ideal humanity and the real thing, and choosing the real thing.

In Abraham humanity says to God, 'There is nothing more important than you. I will give up my whole world to be with you.' In Jesus, God says to humanity, 'There is nothing more important than you. I will give up everything to be with you.'

For all her scathing remarks about those who can't see her condition truthfully, my friend Kate has found companions who recognize the horror. 'Some people', she says, 'give you their heartbreak like a gift. One time my favourite nurse sat down next to me at the cancer clinic and said softly: "I've been meaning to tell you. I lost a baby."' Kate goes on, 'The way she said "baby" with the lightest touch, made me understand. She had nurtured a spark of life in her body and held that child in her arms, and somewhere along the way she had been forced to bury that piece of herself in the ground.'

The cross of Jesus isn't for minimizing, lesson-finding, or solving. Like Kate's condition, it's all consuming, bewildering, indescribable. But the story of Abraham and Isaac, like the nurse's soft intervention, helps us understand. God says, 'There is nothing more important than you', that we might say so too.

5

Sacrifice

The book of Esther is set in the fifth century BC, among Jews in Susa, the capital of the Persian Empire, which ruled a vast territory, including the land of Israel. The Jew Esther has become queen, but her cousin Mordechai has antagonized the chief minister, Haman, so much that Haman contrives to pass a decree that all the Jews in the Empire will be exterminated in a few months' time. The only way to stop this is for Esther to petition the king to pass a contrary law. But this can only be done at great risk, because no one, even the queen, may speak to the king except at his request. Esther has to bring about circumstances where he makes such a request. By placing her life in such danger, and thus saving her entire people, Esther comes closer than anyone in the Old Testament to representing Christ. Here Mordechai persuades Esther to take up her cross.

Then Esther spoke to Hathach and gave him a message for Mordecai, saying, 'All the king's servants and the people of the king's provinces know that if any man or woman goes to the king inside the inner court without being called, there is but one law – all alike are to be put to death. Only if the king holds out the golden sceptre to someone, may that person live. I myself have not been called to come in to the king for thirty days.' When they told Mordecai what Esther had said, Mordecai told them to reply to Esther, 'Do not think that in the king's palace you will escape any more than all the other Jews. For if you keep silence at such a time as this, relief and deliverance will rise for the Jews from another quarter, but you and your father's family will perish. Who knows? Perhaps you have come to royal dignity for just such a time as this.' Then Esther said in reply to Mordecai, 'Go, gather all the Jews to be found in Susa, and hold a fast on my behalf, and neither eat nor drink for three days, night or day. I and my maids will also fast as you do. After that I will go to the king, though it is against the law; and if I perish, I perish.' (Esther 4.10–16)

The broadcaster and author Melvyn Bragg grew up on the north-west coast of Cumbria. His novel *A Soldier's Return* tells the story of Sam, a lieutenant in the British army in Burma during the Far Eastern campaign of the Second World War. There are two settings for the novel. The first is a Cumbrian market town in the mid-1940s, where Sam tries with great difficulty to settle back into the rhythms of work and family life. The second is Burma two or three years earlier, to which Sam's mind and the narrative of the novel frequently return in flashbacks – flashbacks that explain why settling back into mundane provincial life is such a challenge.

Sam tries to deal with his inner turmoil by writing letters to the families of his soldiers who lost their lives during the fighting in Burma. Because his regiment all came from Cumbria, Sam has the opportunity to visit some of the families. Thus Sam visits Mr and Mrs Bell, whose son Ian had been a member of Sam's company. Sam sits down at their house to an inevitably awkward tea, and begins to explain to Mr and Mrs Bell what a terrific soldier Ian had been. Sam goes on to say that Ian talked a great deal about his family, that he'd deeply cared about them and had missed them terribly. Sam says a lot of kind things about Ian – that he was courageous, that everyone liked him, that he was always eager to give others a helping hand. Then the time comes for Sam to talk about the way Ian died. Sam goes over again the things he'd expressed when he first wrote to Mr and Mrs Bell. A sniper had taken Ian out: his death was sudden and instantaneous, in the midst of combat.

Ian hadn't felt anything – he'd been killed in a flash. Silence hangs in the room until Mrs Bell takes herself back to the kitchen. The two men stay in silence as they finished their tea. There isn't anything to say.

Finally Mr Bell takes the initiative, and, putting on a hat and a jacket, gestures to Sam it's time to get some fresh air. Sam wheels his bike beside Mr Bell as they make their way through the village. Then Mr Bell starts to make a path toward the sea across the sand dunes, and Sam pushes his bike with more difficulty up a hill. Once they reach the top of the hill Mr Bell sets his face toward Scotland, and Sam stands beside him, the bike in between them. They share a moment to light a cigarette. Mr Bell talks about his time in the First World War, in the medical corps. He makes it clear he didn't believe in killing; but he wasn't scared. His role was to bring back from no-man's land the charred remains of the bodies the battle left behind. Time and again he'd witnessed a horrifying sight: looking over and again into what was left of a face, he'd become accustomed to throwing up.

All of which is a preliminary to what Mr Bell says next. It's clear he understands that Sam's story is an attempt to be kind. He says straightforwardly to Sam that he wants to know what really happened to his son Ian. But he doesn't turn round to look at Sam as he speaks. Sam isn't ready for Mr Bell's piercing honesty. Through the swirling wind, and speaking to the back of Mr Bell, Sam begins telling a different story. It had been a good day. They'd been in an open patch of land in Burma, in a forest clearing. As he talks, Sam has the image in his mind as vivid as the beach below. There'd been no danger. The Japanese were a long way off. The company was spending the time taking stock and the soldiers were mending their gear. Ian was one of the tidy ones. Sam recalls being a yard away from him. There were plenty of men close by and strewn all over the clearing, tending to their equipment. It was a rare relaxed few days when the enemy wasn't breathing down their throats.

Sam hadn't forgotten a single detail. He saw Ian with a smile and a fag poking out of his mouth, and a dreamy, happy look on his face, completely self-contained – but still sharp enough to realize his lieutentant wanted a cigarette and generous enough to throw him a packet, before resuming his cleaning regime. And then the moment came. Ian was cleaning a grenade. No one would ever understand why. Sam struggles to put this into words. All the moisture drains from his mouth as he's speaking. Ian had taken out the pin of the grenade before he'd pulled out the fuse. Why he'd done it, what he imagined he was doing, would forever remain a mystery. There was only one outcome. Five seconds later the grenade would explode.

Just as Mr Bell can never forget the faces of those he retrieved from no man's land in the Great War, Sam can never forget the look on Ian's face at that moment. Both men knew straightaway that there was no escape. Surrounded as he was for a hundred yards in each direction by his fellow soldiers, there was nowhere that Ian could throw the grenade without causing carnage. Ian looked open-eyed and open-mouthed, and then, to Sam's astonishment, Ian's face had broken into a gentle, sweet smile. He started to speak; but all of a sudden he doubled over and smothered the grenade with his body, taking into himself the whole force of the explosion. Yet he lived for a further two hours. He didn't scream, but from time to time he simply whimpered, 'Sorry!' How could you step aside from such a sound and such a sight?

With hesitation and careful silences Sam tells Mr Bell the whole story. Mr Bell buckles as if he'd been struck, and leans forward in a convulsion as it were to be sick. Then he steadies himself, and announces he won't be telling Ian's mother, since she's only just managing with what she knows. Sam realizes the conversation is at an end. He pushes his bike towards the road. When he looks behind him, Mr Bell is stood to attention, ready to face whatever ensues.[1]

---

1 Melvyn Bragg, *A Soldier's Return*, Arcade, 2003, pp. 114–17.

Each of the three men in this story knew intimately about sacrifice. The first, Ian, never came back from the war. The second, Sam, did come back but had lost everything. The novel is really about Sam. It's about what happens when you've lost your stomach and your heart but you begin trying to live again. The third character, Mr Bell, stayed in England but his life without his son would never be the same again. So one never came back; one came back but lost everything; one stayed but would never be the same. Each knew all about sacrifice.

I want to suggest to you that the story of Ian, Sam and Mr Bell can be read as a story about God, about the cross, and as a modern-day Esther story. When Ian looks around the camp and realizes that there's nowhere he can throw the grenade, he shows us the face of Christ. Within the ghastly carnage and destruction of war, we catch this glimpse of what and who Jesus is. Jesus is the one who lays down his life so that all may live. Ian experiences in his own body the price of human folly and failure. Why does the pin come out of the grenade? We don't really know. Why does humanity find itself at enmity with itself and at enmity with God? We don't really know. Almost every explanation really comes down to a description of the symptoms. But that the grenade is ticking away, that what we have set loose stands to do untold damage to us and to all creation – that's undeniable: that we know very well. And here is Ian, here is Christ, bent double over the force that threatens to obliterate us, laying down his life that we might be saved. That's what Esther does. She takes upon herself the full weight of what it means to save the entire Jewish people. Esther is the closest the Old Testament gets to a portrayal of Jesus.

And in Sam we see God the comforter just as strongly represented. Sam is the one who as the commanding officer represented a kind of parent to Ian. Now, back in Cumbria, he represents Ian to Ian's parents. And uncannily Mr and Mrs Bell see Ian in Sam, and Sam sees Ian in Mr and Mrs Bell. Sam makes his parents present to Ian and makes Ian present to his parents. Sam is the bearer of two stories: the story that Ian died as part of a war that was finally won – the story he tells to Mrs Bell; and the story that Ian died through stupidity and carelessness and folly and in the end through an act of courageous sacrifice that can only evoke awe and astonishment – the story Sam tells to Mr Bell. Sam gives us a picture of the Holy Spirit – the comforter, the one who makes Christ present, the one who offers the face of Christ to the Father and the face of the Father to Christ, the one who breathes into life the story of salvation.

And in Mr Bell we see what it means to lose your only son. In Mr Bell we see what it means to carry in your heart two stories about what your son's death means. The first story is a story of glory, a story in which Ian's death is part of a great achievement, in this case victory in Burma, success in the Far East campaign, peace in our time. The second story is one of folly, no enemy anywhere near, a happy lazy sunny afternoon, a careless lapse in attention, and a breathtaking moment of agonizing courage. In Mr Bell we see God the Father, whose only Son dies on the cross through a mixture of God's indescribable love and our unspeakable folly. These two profound truths remain in the Father's heart for ever.

Many of us want to tell an angry story about the world and our lives, rather like the story Mr Bell tells about the First World War – a story of mismanaged resources, of unjust relations where hundreds of poor people die to sustain the lifestyle of their richer compatriots, a story of brutality and cruelty and fear. Others of us want to tell a more idealized story of our lives, rather like the story Sam tells Mrs Bell about Ian, a story of inevitable setbacks on the rolling march to freedom, truth and glory. But the figure we most need to reckon with on Good Friday is not Mr Bell or Sam. It's Ian. The pin is out of the grenade. Whether through perversity or ignorance, we are sinners. The pin is out of the grenade, like it or not. We have two options. One is to put as much distance as we can between ourselves and the grenade, whoever else the grenade might damage or destroy. But that wasn't Ian's way. Ian's way was to take the destruction in his own body and in doing so to save the life of others. Ian's way was to lose his life to gain it, to let his grain of wheat fall so it might bear much fruit. Ian is a modern-day Esther – and a twentieth-century Christ.

Ian shows us the only way to redeem the horror of the worst violence the world can generate. He turns his whole body into the shape it needs to be to make his companions' life possible. He makes the worst horror into something beautiful. This is how he imitates Christ: by shaping his body so as to give us life. This is how he models the life of the church: a body shaped to bring life to others. This is what the church asks of us: to shape our abundant resources to give life to the world. What Mordecai says to Esther he may be saying to all of us: perhaps we have been sent, right here, right now, for just such a time as this.

Faith means dealing with Mrs Bell's fantasy with compassion and patience, recognizing Mr Bell's half-truth with humility and integrity, and aspiring to Sam's faltering honesty with courage and hope. It's not always, at every moment, about the searing honesty of the final conversation between Sam and Mr Bell. But in the arms of the heartbroken Father, in the grace of the sacrificial Son, and in the fellowship of the comforting Spirit, we face the death of such conversations, knowing that true resurrection cannot be found any other way.

6

Passover

The crucifixion of Jesus took place at Passover. The early Christians came to see that as central to its meaning. For them, it summed up the church's relationship with Israel. Passover links together the three great themes of the Old Testament: God is the liberator who sets Israel free, a freedom represented by the parting of the Red Sea; God sets Israel free for a reason: God says, 'You are to be my friends', and this friendship is represented by the covenant made with Moses on Mount Sinai; and this setting-free-for-friendship God is none other than the creator God, the maker of heaven and earth, who established the whole creation for this central purpose. So Passover is about the creator, the liberator and the sanctifier. On the night before he died Jesus identified himself closely with the Passover. By saying, 'This is my body', Jesus was announcing, 'Everything the Passover means, I mean.' Jesus is God passing over our sins and setting us free.

The Lord said to Moses and Aaron, 'Tell the whole congregation of Israel that on the tenth of this month they are to take a lamb for each family. Your lamb shall be without blemish, a year-old male; you may take it from the sheep or from the goats. You shall keep it until the fourteenth day of this month; then the whole assembled congregation of Israel shall slaughter it at twilight. They shall take some of the blood and put it on the two doorposts and the lintel of the houses in which they eat it. They shall eat the lamb that same night; they shall eat it roasted over the fire with unleavened bread and bitter herbs. This is how you shall eat it: your loins girded, your sandals on your feet, and your staff in your hand; and you shall eat it hurriedly. It is the passover of the Lord. For I will pass through the land of Egypt that night, and I will strike down every firstborn in the land of Egypt, both human beings and animals; on all the gods of Egypt I will execute judgements: I am the Lord. The blood shall be a sign for you on the houses where you live: when I see the blood, I will pass over you, and no plague shall destroy you when I strike the land of Egypt. (Exodus 12.1–13, abridged)

Imagine the scene in Jerusalem in the days following Palm Sunday. 250,000 lambs clustering into gateways, bursting down tight passageways, pouring into close barns and shelters. Each lamb was set to furnish one Passover meal. At least ten people were required for each meal. Which means around 2 million people teeming through the holy places and cheap hotels of Jerusalem, squabbling over tent space on the Mount of Olives, and all searching for bread, water, and ingredients for the great meal.[1]

Imagine, if you can bear it, the scene in the Temple. Every single householder brings his lamb and kills it with his own hands, yet doesn't strangle it. Two long lines of priests receive the blood of each slaughtered lamb in a cup, then pass it up the line till it's splashed on the altar, and flows out down pipes into the River Kedron, which turns into a red moving sludge. The lamb is hung, skinned and opened, then carried home and carefully roasted. Think of the smell, the noise, the chaos. All this is contained in Mark's simple words 'they prepared the Passover meal.'

And then move from the pandemonium of the Temple to the relative quiet of the upper room. The upper room was the guest-chamber, constructed either permanently or temporarily

---

1 This account is indebted to Matthew Byrne, *The Day He Died: The Passion according to Luke*, Columba Books, 2004.

on the flat roof of a house. The guest-room that Jesus had booked was a large one, big enough for the 13 people who would share supper together. It was by no means the first meal the 13 had shared together, for there were a number of other meals at which Jesus revealed different aspects of his character and saving purpose.

And in the centre of the circle on the table would have been the four ceremonial cups of wine, the brick-shaped concoction of fruits, nuts and vinegar representing the bricks the Hebrews made in Egypt, the bitter herbs representing slavery, the unleavened bread representing their hasty departure, and the lamb itself, whose blood sprinkled on the doorposts delivered the Hebrews from the angel of death.

The host blesses the first cup and all drink. Then comes the bitter herbs, which are blessed and eaten. Then the bread, the dried fruit and the lamb are brought in. The second cup is poured, and the story of the Israel's exodus from Egypt and crossing of the Red Sea is told. The second cup is drunk and the bread is broken. The host blesses the bread mixed with herbs and fruit and eats it along with some of the lamb, saying, 'This is the body of the Passover.' All feast. Then they drink the third cup and say some psalms before drinking the fourth cup.

At least, this is what is supposed to happen. But on this occasion, the host is Jesus. After the second cup Jesus takes the bread, offers the thanksgiving, breaks it and distributes it. And instead of saying, 'This is the body of the Passover', he says, 'This is my body.' And when the time comes to take the third cup, Jesus says, 'This is my blood.' And he adds, 'I will never again drink of the fruit of the vine until that day when I drink it new in the kingdom of God.'

When Jesus says, 'The broken bread is my broken body; the poured wine is my shed blood', he's inviting us to see the crucifixion and the Eucharist as the same thing. The taking of the bread and wine is a prefigurement and a portrayal of the cross. We've just heard Abraham striding up the mountain with his son Isaac, and Isaac saying, 'Here are the fire and the wood, but where is the lamb for the sacrifice?' We've heard Abraham reply, in words of multiple resonance and irony, 'God will provide the lamb for the sacrifice, my son.' You can imagine the disciples saying, 'Here are the bitter herbs and the dried fruit, but where is the Passover lamb?' None of the gospels explicitly mentions the lamb. Why? Because you can almost hear Jesus saying, 'God will provide the lamb for the sacrifice, my beloved children'. The Eucharist celebrates that God did provide for Abraham, and does provide for us. And what God provides is, of course, Jesus – the Lamb of God: Jesus, the sacrificial lamb whose death is the end of sacrifice, who died that the Kedron River and every other river the world over no longer be a red moving sludge. These are the moments we place at the centre of our Christian faith: the body broken so that we may be united with God, the blood poured so that no blood might ever be poured again. The Eucharist is the cross of Christ.

But when Jesus said, 'This is my body', he wasn't just referring to his crucified body. He was also referring to his resurrected body. People often discuss whether and in what form Jesus really rose from the dead – whether his resurrection body was broadly the same or completely different from the body that was crucified. But the transformation in Jesus' body does not begin on Holy Saturday: it begins when Jesus says, 'This is my body.' My body is people making and renewing friendship with God and one another. My body is people learning to want the things God gives us in plenty, and discovering that God gives them everything they need. My body is people voluntarily facing the cost of discipleship and pouring out love on the way of the cross. And all these parts of my body centre on one definitive moment, the resurrection of my body on Easter Day. Glory, life eternal, the everlasting presence of God and our finding our true home in the life of the Trinity: these are all ways of rendering permanent the joy of the resurrection of Jesus' body. And that lasting joy is most frequently portrayed as a banquet, a constant sharing of the bread of everyday life and the wine of eternal life. That banquet is a constant moment of worship, of companionship, and of sharing food. It's what we call heaven. The Eucharist is resurrection: a moment of heaven on earth.

So when he said, 'This is my body', Jesus depicted the significance of the cross and anticipated the heaven his resurrection would bring. But we must never forget the circumstances in which he said these words. He was being betrayed by one disciple, about to be denied by another, and deserted by the rest. All around was the chaos of a religious festival and the stench of the slaughtered lambs. This was no sentimental piety, no tasteful, cosy and comfortable evening in with friends. And so we shouldn't expect our Eucharists to be cosy and comfortable, tasteful and sentimental. If our country is in turmoil, our community in distress, our personal life in tatters and international politics in disgrace, we may share the Eucharist in good company, for such was the situation on the day Christ's body was broken.

So next time you attend the Eucharist one Sunday, and later that day you speak to a friend and they say, 'How was church this morning?', you may reply, 'Oh, it brought me face to face with the cross of Christ; it made me free for friendship with God and others; and it was a prefigurement of heaven on earth: otherwise, nothing special, I suppose.' And all of this is contained in the moment Jesus took bread, and said, 'This is my body.'

7

Atonement

Perhaps the most catastrophic day in the story the Old Testament tells came in 585 BC, when the Babylonians captured Jerusalem. Thereafter the people of Judah, the southern kingdom that had survived the fall of the north 140 years previously, awaited one of two fates. Some were destroyed, either by death or by their culture and identity being eradicated in the decades that followed; others went into exile in Babylon, a thousand miles away. Those who sought to make sense of what had happened largely concluded that it was God's judgement on the sin of a people who, after the covenant with David and the building of the Temple under Solomon, had spent the subsequent 400 years straying from God's ways. And just as the book of Leviticus speaks of two goats, one of which was slaughtered and the other sent away into the wilderness, so it's hard not to see echoes in the two fates of Judah, some destroyed and some sent away to Babylon. These, it seems, are the two ways God deals with sin.

The Lord said to Moses: 'Your brother Aaron shall take from the congregation of the people of Israel two male goats for a sin-offering, and one ram for a burnt-offering. Aaron shall make atonement for himself and for his house. He shall take the two goats and set them before the Lord at the entrance of the tent of meeting; and Aaron shall cast lots on the two goats, one lot for the Lord and the other lot for Azazel. Aaron shall present the goat on which the lot fell for the Lord, and offer it as a sin-offering; but the goat on which the lot fell for Azazel shall be presented alive before the Lord to make atonement over it, so that it may be sent away into the wilderness to Azazel.

He shall slaughter the goat of the sin-offering that is for the people and bring its blood inside the curtain, sprinkling it upon the mercy-seat and before the mercy-seat. Then he shall lay both his hands on the head of the live goat, and confess over it all the iniquities of the people of Israel, and all their transgressions, all their sins, putting them on the head of the goat, and sending it away into the wilderness by means of someone designated for the task. The goat shall bear on itself all their iniquities to a barren region; and the goat shall be set free in the wilderness. (Leviticus 16.2, 6–9, 15, 21–22)

Leviticus 16 speaks in uncompromising terms about the elaborate methods by which God ordains and Israel conducts the regular process of making atonement for sin. The heart of the ritual is the slaying of an animal on whose head is taken to rest all the sins of the people. By the ungrudging yielding of its first-fruits and through obedient faithfulness to God's instructions, Israel is cleansed of its iniquities and God remembers its sin no more.

But tucked into this comprehensive prescription for redemption lies a fascinating alternative model. One goat gets the slit-throat and burnt-carcass treatment. But the other goat has hands laid upon it, as if in a parody of blessing, and is sent out into the wilderness to become what we have come to call a scapegoat – an 'escape' goat. The goat escapes death, and we escape judgement.

Now there's much confusion about this scapegoat. A host of psychologists, philosophers and anthropologists see the origin of culture and religion in the infectious escalation of desire, caused by the fact that we don't create our own desires, we instead learn to long for what everyone else longs for. This escalation leads to tension, because not everyone can acquire the desired things, and that tension leads to conflict. This conflict results in a conflagration of competition and violence. How does such violence end? This is where the scapegoat comes in. Over and again it seems the founding myth of many cultures involve a perceived outsider being identified, like a witch, as the source of all evil, and that outsider consequently being put to death by the community. The war of all against all is transformed into the unity of all against one. The cathartic death of this victim dissipates the desire, assuages the crisis and thus restores peace. That ensuing peace vindicates and sacralizes the whole process. Thus Oedipus transgresses natural law by sleeping with his mother and killing his father; once he is blinded and expelled, peace returns to Thebes. Romulus and Remus found Rome, but Remus transgresses by jumping over the furrow that marked where the walls would be built, so he has to die and peace returns.

For these thinkers this story of mimetic violence and scapegoating is false. The Bible challenges this conventional way of making peace through identifying, isolating and punishing a victim, because in the Christian story the victim, Jesus, is innocent. Thus the death of Jesus both exposes and discredits the whole notion of victimization. Interestingly the founder of this school of thought, René Girard, first established his theory of mimetic desire and violence and then became a Christian when he realized how the Bible story runs so profoundly counter to it.

But I'm not sure this tradition reads the Leviticus instructions for the two goats very closely. What it seems to miss is that in Leviticus the scapegoat is a form of mercy. The scapegoat isn't a victim, in a conventional way. It's certainly not the focus of cathartic violence. It isn't slaughtered. It's let go, albeit into the wilderness. But, as Israel eventually returned from exile in Babylon, so too can the goat in due time return from the wilderness. In other words the scapegoat is originally a form of mercy as much as judgement.

The perfect example of this is the story of Joseph, mostly famous for his technicolor dreamcoat. The ten brothers turn on him out of envy, insecurity and hatred, and intend to kill him, but instead sell him to some Ishmaelites heading towards Egypt, and interestingly kill a goat and present its blood on the dreamcoat to give Jacob the impression that Joseph has been killed in the wilderness.

All of which is telling us Jesus is not just the sacrificial goat who is slaughtered, and whose blood constitutes our atonement. Jesus is also the other goat, the scapegoat, the one who is sent away into the wilderness and who identifies with all who are cast out by their own people because those people believe they will be made pure by rejecting one of their number. When Jesus says the words, 'My God, my God, why have you forsaken me?', he's indicating that he's been cast out not just by the Romans, not just by the Jerusalem authorities, not just by the crowds, not just by the disciples, but also by the Father. What makes Jesus a scapegoat is not so much that he's the sacrificial victim – that's what the first goat represents – but more that he's ostracized, humiliated, deserted, and ultimately, utterly, cosmically alone.

The question then is whether Jesus fulfils the Old Testament by replacing one elaborate, legal, ritual and apparently unfair form of atonement with another, or whether Jesus transcends these complex and troubling forms of justice by something beyond justice.

I got close to an answer to this question a few months ago. I was in my office when the phone rang. The voice said, simply, 'Sam.' And instantly I was transported back in time. A familiar voice, with a strong regional accent; just one word was instantly recognizable after decades without contact. He was a firefighter. He started coming to church about the time I began in the parish. He was in my first adult confirmation class. I sat down intently.

'I heard you on the radio this morning and thought I'd leave a message – I never expected you to pick up the phone,' said my long-lost parishioner. We caught up for fifteen minutes until I felt I should be doing something else. Ten minutes later the phone rang. It was him again. 'I was so surprised you picked up I forgot what I really meant to say. I have a confession to make.' I paused. 'Well,' I said, 'I'm in the business. Take your time.' He didn't seem too daunted, for a man about to bare his soul. 'Do you remember your first Easter at St Luke's?' What a wonderful question. It was 1992. I was overjoyed to be in the thick of parish life. But what did he mean? 'Two weeks before Easter at the Sunday service you gave each one of us three nails. You said, 'Put these somewhere where you'll be close to them every day. And on Easter morning, bring them back with you and put them in the font and celebrate what those nails really mean.'

By the time he'd finished I was thinking, 'Hmmm, I used to do that kind of thing. I've almost forgotten.' But I said, 'How 'bout that. Tell me about your confession.' He said, 'The truth is, I never brought the nails back.' This is the point where, if it's a face to face conversation, you look over your glasses and say nothing and just make an encouraging nod to indicate you're really listening. But on the phone you can't do that, so I said, 'Go on.'

'When I took the nails home,' he said, 'I knew what I wanted to do. The next day, I took them to the fire station. I picked up my firefighter's overalls and I sewed each one of them into its own pocket across my chest. And then I gave each one of them a name. 'The first one, the largest one, I called Faith. The second one, the rusty one, I called Courage. And the third one, the twisted, almost broken one, I called Hope. And from then on, for the next 20 years, every time the bell went and we jumped down the chute into the fire tender to go out on a job, I would put my hand on my chest. My hand would cover the pocket with the first nail, and I would say, 'Be close to me, I need you with me.' I would move across to the second nail, and would say, 'Give me the strength to do what I need to do today.' And then I'd find the third, twisted, smaller nail, and I'd say, 'Help me make it through to live another day. I kept those three nails in my overalls until six years ago when I retired. And when I heard your voice on the radio I thought it was time to tell you why I never brought them back that Easter Day.'

I was silent about as long as you can be silent on the phone without making your companion nervous. I was in awe.

As I look back on that conversation I think about what the nails mean and what the two goats mean. The first goat is saying, if there's something wrong, find the source of the problem or at least the symbolic focus of the problem and destroy it. The second goat is saying, extract the venom of the problem and saddle it on some kind of a vehicle and send that vehicle away as far as you can, out of sight and out of mind. But my firefighter parishioner perceived that neither of these are finally the way God addresses what's wrong. In Jesus God dons the overalls of our flesh. Though we are tough and sharp as nails, Jesus painstakingly sews us into God's heart. God doesn't deal with sin and death by achieving solutions at arm's length. Instead we are taken into God's heart, broken, twisted and rusty as we are.

8

Servant

Isaiah marks the turning point in the Old Testament. Up to this point Israel sees God as the one who, with faithful adherence to the covenant, will bring blessings now and forever. Sin and iniquity will be punished. But in the central chapters of Isaiah, especially Isaiah 53, Israel comes to understand that God embodies this covenant so deeply that sin and evil damage not just Israel but also God. God can suffer. And that suffering arises from love. God is in the end not judge, but lover. And God will go to any lengths to restore that love.

(1) My servant shall prosper; he shall be exalted and shall be very high. Many were astonished at him – so marred was his appearance, beyond human semblance. He shall startle many nations; for that which had not been told them they shall see.

(2) Who has believed what we have heard?

(3) He had no form or majesty that we should look at him or desire him. He was despised and rejected by others; a man of suffering and acquainted with infirmity; as one from whom others hide their faces he was despised, and we held him of no account.

(4) Surely he has borne our infirmities. Yet we accounted him struck down by God, and afflicted. But he was wounded for our transgressions, crushed for our iniquities; upon him was the punishment that made us whole, and by his bruises we are healed. All we like sheep have gone astray; we have all turned to our own way, and the Lord has laid on him the iniquity of us all.

(5) He was oppressed, and he was afflicted, yet he did not open his mouth; like a lamb that is led to the slaughter, and like a sheep that before its shearers is silent, so he did not open his mouth. By a perversion of justice he was taken away. Who could have imagined his future? For he was cut off from the land of the living, stricken for the transgression of my people. They made his grave with the wicked although he had done no violence, and there was no deceit in his mouth.

(6) Yet it was the will of the Lord to crush him with pain. Through him the will of the Lord shall prosper. Out of his anguish he shall see light and knowledge.

(7) The righteous one, my servant, shall make many righteous, and he shall bear their iniquities. Therefore I will allot him a portion with the great, because he poured out himself to death, and was numbered with the transgressors; yet he bore the sin of many, and made intercession for the transgressors. (Isaiah 52.13—53.12 abridged)

After five decades on earth and three decades of ministry I've come to the conclusion that there are broadly three ways to live. The first is to seek with all one's heart and strength to avoid pain, discomfort, hardship, disease and disappointment and to maximize pleasure, security, longevity and distraction. The second is to jettison ease and fulfilment and to seek to enhance the benefit, well-being and flourishing of others. The third is to set aside the anxiety of mortality, the superficial esteem of others and the panacea of distraction and look deeply and unflinchingly into the mystery of existence, refusing to glance away when what you see is uninviting or unpalatable.

It's no exaggeration to say that for Christians Isaiah 53 is the most significant passage in the Old Testament. It's almost impossible to comprehend Jesus' passion without reading it through the magnifying glass of this chapter of Isaiah. There are two conventional ways to read Isaiah 53. The first is to say the prophet had no notion of a saviour figure like Jesus and was almost certainly referring to an idealized Israel emerging out of its period of exile in Babylon in a renewed mission to be God's servant. The second is to say every aspect of Jesus' passion exactly fulfilled this remarkable prophecy and anyone who can't see that is wilfully obtuse. Both of these approaches seem to miss the almost certain fact that Jesus knew these words well and they were written on his heart from childhood. When you grasp that, you realize the passion narratives in the gospels were written by people who had come to understand that Jesus went to Jerusalem consciously obeying a call to embody these words.

But people still tend to read Isaiah 53 in the light of which of the three ways to live they've adopted. For those for who life is about achieving comfort and security, Isaiah 53 is a puzzle made up of poetic words and allusive references. The clue to the puzzle is to perceive that the servant is Jesus, that he underwent great hardship and cruelty, and that the result was the forgiveness of sin and life with God forever. I believe all of that is in the chapter but I don't think Isaiah's words are like a code we simply decipher and thus gain salvation now and forever, because that treats Jesus' passion like a get out of jail card in a Monopoly game. For those who believe in serving others, Isaiah 53 is an illustration of what we already know, that we should put others' needs before our own and to make a better world requires noble sacrifice, selfless dedication and a very thick skin. But that makes Isaiah 53 not much more than an ancient and glorified version of Rudyard Kipling's 'If'.

For me Isaiah 53 needs to be read in a desire to look deeply and unflinchingly into the mystery of existence. That means letting go of an urge to make it all fit some kind of formula of salvation or illustrate some kind of virtuous moral behaviour. The chapter comes in seven sections, and, like some other celebrated passages of Old Testament poetry, they form a chiasmus, with the first section mirroring the last, the second mirroring the sixth, the third the fifth, and the fourth section being thus highlighted as the one in the middle, the point of the arrow. What the whole poem is saying is, this is the heart of existence – this is the nature of God's character. And if you want to perceive the mystery of all things, you need to align yourself with the heart of God and the true nature of all things. So let's look at what it says.

The beginning and end of the poem, sections 1 and 7, gather together three apparently contradictory things: this is about a person who is disfigured, despised and rejected; whose story is almost universally misunderstood; and yet who is finally vindicated and whose truth prevails over all other truth. That's the intriguing mystery into which this poem invites us.

The next parts, sections 2 and 6, deepen that sense of confusion and misunderstanding. They acknowledge that no one can believe this story. They affirm paradoxical convictions – that though this person is close to God, God nonetheless consents to this person being crushed with pain; that though this seems so troubling, nonetheless the Lord's will shall emerge from it; and that the person themselves will emerge with wisdom and insight.

The next dimension, sections 3 and 5, intensify the sense of alienation and violence directed at the person. Here are some of the most resonant words of the passion: despised, rejected, a man of suffering and acquainted with infirmity; oppressed and afflicted, yet he did not open his mouth; like a lamb led to the slaughter, like a sheep silent before its shearers; he was cut off from the land of the living. They made his grave with the wicked. It was a perversion of justice.

All of this sets up and exalts the central assertions of section 4. He has borne our infirmities, was wounded for our transgressions, crushed for our iniquities; by his bruises we are healed. We like sheep have gone astray and turned to our own way. The Lord has laid on him the iniquity of us all. In other words, everyone thought he was suffering for what he'd done wrong. But it turns out he was suffering for what others had done wrong. His suffering brings them to restoration. God has worked through this and blessed it all. The presence of God, the experience of suffering, and the incomprehension of those watching are all wrapped with one another. This is the mystery at the heart of existence. This is the mystery of Good Friday.

If we stay with this mystery through and beyond its unpalatable dimensions, this is what it's telling us. There can be a profound dignity in the rejected. When we're rejected we can find a deeper identity than the simple desire to belong and be accepted. There can be real truth in pain. When we're in pain it's not always simply a quick fix to take the pain away: that pain may be showing us something about fragility, connectedness, patience, endurance. Injustice is wrong, but there can be some times when we must find ways to carry grief, punishment, constraint that is not our fault or of our own making. Being despised is humiliating and wounding, but there is also sometimes wisdom and grace in saying nothing and relying on example and demeanour. Suffering is all-consuming and defeating, but it can yet yield wisdom and recognition. These are things that people who've gone to the heart of it all know, these are things that are found deep in the heart of God; but seem absurd to those for whom life is about comfort and security alone. Good Friday isn't a magic trick by which Jesus used the special formula to produce the genie of salvation out of the bottle of sin and death. It's the day on which Jesus went into the cloud of unknowing and the tunnel of despair and the chamber of agony to show that God being with us is the heart of it all.

The 2016 film *Hacksaw Ridge* tells the true story of the Seventh Day Adventist Desmond Doss. In childhood Desmond almost kills his younger brother. He also almost shoots his drunken father, who threatens his mother with a gun. These experiences make him a pacifist. Nonetheless he enrols in the US army after Pearl Harbor. He's a mystery to his fellow soldiers, because he trains well but won't handle a gun. He's beaten and tortured by his colleagues who try to make him leave or change his mind. The authorities also humiliate him, trying and failing to get him thrown out on psychiatric grounds.

In spring 1945 Desmond's unit is deployed to the Battle

of Okinawa, and ordered to ascend and secure the massive edifice of Hacksaw Ridge. As a medical orderly, Desmond enters the heat of battle, and under heavy fire he finds and rescues one wounded soldier after another. When the Japanese counter attack, the American forces are driven off the cliff. Only Desmond is left, and by courage, strength and subterfuge he time and again returns to haul the wounded to the cliff edge where they are stretchered down the massive descent to safety. Finally he saves the commanding officer who tried at boot camp to get him court martialled. When all the stretchers are counted, this mysterious figure, despised, rejected and abused, this man who was oppressed and afflicted but never opened his mouth, this person from whom others hid their faces and held of no account had saved no fewer than 75 soldiers, carrying every single one out of the mire of conflict and under the hail of gunfire and sending them down a 300-foot escarpment by rope and pulley.

Hacksaw Ridge could simply be a hero tale of rescue and glory. But that wouldn't do justice to who Desmond Doss was. It could be an inspiring story of laying down your life for others, but again it's more subtle than that. Desmond Doss entered the mystery of God by refusing to take up arms yet at the same time putting himself on the front line of conflict. Like the servant of Isaiah 53 he faced total incomprehension, violent hostility, virulent ostracism, and yet a profound sense of God's call and blessing. And like Isaiah's servant, he was vindicated, and all the things everyone previously thought to be true and wise and certain were unravelled, and he brought friend and stranger, enemy and despiser into the mystery of the living God.

PART 3

The Cross in the Epistles

Somewhat to my surprise, I found that the word 'cross' only appears in the New Testament epistles around half a dozen times. So this section considers those references, scattered across several letters. This part of the book was written in the context of the coronavirus. But the virus largely intensified the issues humanity was already facing. So rather than consider what the cross has to say to the virus, this section reflects on what these six images tell us about the cross today.

9

Forgiveness: Who's Forgiving Whom?

And when you were dead in trespasses and the uncircumcision of your flesh, God made you alive together with him, when he forgave us all our trespasses, erasing the record that stood against us with its legal demands. He set this aside, nailing it to the cross. He disarmed the rulers and authorities and made a public example of them, triumphing over them in it. (Colossians 2.13–15)

Leo Tolstoy's 1869 novel *War and Peace* introduces us to Pierre, the socially awkward, perhaps autistic character at the heart of the novel. He's somewhat innocent, but wastes a lot of his youth in drinking bouts, led on by his pleasure-seeking soldier friend, Ivan. Pierre is one of his father's countless illegitimate sons, but in 1805 inherits the whole of his father's fortune, and becomes a highly eligible bachelor. The first to capitalize is Hélène, a renowned beauty, who contrives to marry him for his money. Finding Hélène loveless, and marriage lonely, Pierre suggests his old friend Ivan move in with them. Before long it's clear the unscrupulous Ivan and the lascivious Hélène are having an affair. Pierre challenges Ivan to a duel, and to his surprise, wounds Ivan badly. In time Ivan returns to his soldiering ways. But Pierre's marriage is damaged beyond repair.

Seven years later, in 1812, Pierre is in Moscow when Napoleon invades the city. Pierre stands up for an Armenian family being abused by soldiers and is thrown in prison, narrowly escaping execution. When Napoleon retreats from Moscow, Pierre is among the prisoners taken on the long death-march back to Europe. After several months of hardship and fierce cold, the bedraggled company of soldiers and prisoners is ambushed by a Russian raiding party. At the moment he's freed, Pierre sees the face of the ambush leader. It's his old adversary, Ivan. They shake hands, and the ironies, hurts, regrets and betrayals of the past dissolve in the snow. The friend Pierre had shot for stealing his wife had now reappeared to save his life. There's no alternative to forgiveness. Ivan lives to fight, drink, and sleep around. It's as pointless to condemn him for one as to commend him for another. Pierre's naïve, clumsy and easily manipulated. It's as useless to pity him when he's humiliated as it is to idealize him when he gets lucky. Forgiveness is not so much a grand gesture of reconciliation as a recognition of the interdependence of all our lives, the flaws in all our characters, the complexity of all our motives and the surprises that luck, chance and accident can bring.

The story of Pierre and Ivan vividly demonstrates how deeply betrayal, hurt and estrangement wound our existence, and how easily they lead to violence, death and disaster. But as we examine the work of Christ on the cross, I want to look beyond generalities to identify precisely what's happening in the crucifixion, why it can seem so distant and abstract, and why in the midst of coronavirus it turns out to be truer and more significant than ever.

Look with me again at the story of Pierre and Ivan. You can read it as the story of humanity and God. God has given us a magnificent playground to enjoy. Like Ivan we're called to be trusted and faithful friends, and like Hélène, we're called to be people who make a beautiful society with God. But Ivan and Hélène portray how we manipulate, exploit and disregard God. We ruin our relationship through greed and self-absorption. Pierre is a Christ figure who innocently wanders through Russia seeking the good, albeit in a slightly clumsy way. Pierre's forgiveness of Ivan comes after he has taken on the sins of Russia, on a long march like a via dolorosa from Jerusalem to Golgotha.

But here's what's so different today. I think it's changed even in the last 20 years. It's changed because of four things: the arguments of the New Atheists, the horrors of clergy abuse of children, the church's slowness to reflect society's rapid change in attitudes around sexuality, and the degree to which religion has been identified with global violence and terror. Perhaps you could add the apparent pointlessness of the pandemic. There's been a revolution. Now humanity thinks of itself as Pierre, well-intentioned if a little ham-fisted. But it's started to think of God, or at least the workings of organized religion, as like Hélène and Ivan, distorted, exploitative, malicious, perverse, dangerous, immoral and best avoided – though still capable of offering miraculous rescue in real emergency. Whereas a generation ago a set of Good Friday addresses would have been about the wonder of how God, like Pierre, astonishingly forgives us, today it feels like the real question is whether we can forgive God. The pandemic has only made the issues sharper and more painful.

Seeking to answer this question takes us closer to the heart of the cross than we generally tend to go. Why? Because even though we say we regard Jesus as fully human and fully divine, our imaginations are captivated by the notion of sacrifice. We talk of Jesus' agonizing death in the most vivid terms possible, because we assume God is angry with us, and that anger can only be appeased by a sacrificial lamb. Jesus becomes that lamb and his innocence is imputed to us, so henceforth when God looks on us God sees not our sins but Christ's goodness. Jesus is like the shepherd boy David who comes out of the ranks of Israel and is the one chosen to face the worst nightmare, Goliath, and somehow overcomes that nightmare and brings us freedom, light and peace. Goliath might equate to death. The trouble is, Goliath in the contemporary imagination bears a rather too close resemblance to God. Instead of being our salvation, in the last generation God has come to seem more like Goliath – our blundering, heartless, overbearing enemy.

This is where it changes everything that we see Jesus not just as fully us, but also as fully God. Jesus is not just God forgiving us. Jesus is us forgiving God. If you're going to respond, 'Surely God has given us life, love, laughter, how can we possibly speak of our needing to forgive God?' I'd say, technically you're right, but have you been paying attention these last 20 years? The world is furious with God. It doesn't want to know that God forgives, because it pins on God all the wrongs of life: the horror of abuse, the depredation of the planet, the violence of ideology, the heartlessness of bigotry, the manipulation of the innocent, the catastrophe of the virus. That's what 'God' has come to mean. It's useless and untimely to protest that the sins of the world toward God amount to so much more than that. No one's listening.

So we need to turn the cross round, so it faces in the opposite direction. It's not just our word to God, the word of a holy man to say, 'We've ruined the garden and stolen the fruit, we're sorry, can you forgive us, will this sacrifice of the best-ever man be enough?' Today the cross faces the other way, as God's word to us, and says, 'Will you believe this is my face? I'm not the ghastly Goliath, the belligerent bully, the suffocating, micro-parenting passive-aggressive judge. I'm the one who comes across the acres of eternity, who trudges the tundra of terror, who withstands the distortions of motive and misconstruals of purpose, and holds out in two hands a precious piece of paper, that says, 'You were made for me, to be with me, to flourish and frolic and desire and dance. That's what all this was about. If I or my representatives ever suggested anything else, I'm here to say "sorry"'.

Our question is, will we forgive God? Will we take that piece of paper and hold it to our hearts and embrace the one who bears it? Or will we snatch it from Christ's hands in fury and nail those hands to a cross and punish him for punishing us? Our forebears had that challenge years ago. We have that same challenge today. Can we forgive God, for all the ways our lives are distorted, for all the times religion has gone wrong, for all our own shortcomings and deceptions? Will we receive that paper, that message, that relationship? 'All it was ever about?' Will we see that, through all the confusion of centuries, through all the deceptions and doubts, and look at those pierced hands and realize the message they convey? Here is God, naked, bent, bruised, broken: because that's what it takes to say, 'Will you forgive me?'

10

Obedience: The Nakedness of God

Let the same mind be in you that was in Christ Jesus, who, though he was in the form of God, did not regard equality with God as something to be exploited, but emptied himself, taking the form of a slave, being born in human likeness. And being found in human form, he humbled himself and became obedient to the point of death – even death on a cross. Therefore God also highly exalted him and gave him the name that is above every name, so that at the name of Jesus every knee should bend, in heaven and on earth and under the earth, and every tongue should confess that Jesus Christ is Lord, to the glory of God the Father. (Philippians 2.5–11)

Imagine being a member of a Roman household in the first century AD. There was only one person who mattered: the head of that household. Everyone else, women, girls, boys and slaves, were subject to his demands and desires. Life for many was a perpetual tightrope of danger, distress and degradation. Imagine then that you heard the message of Jesus, in the mouth of an apostle like Paul. 'Your bodies are members of Christ', he said. 'They are a temple of the Holy Spirit', he said. For a prostitute, a prisoner of war, or a slave, this was revolutionary news. Churches were astonishing communities in which race, gender and class were transcended, and power relations transformed. Paul hesitated to dismantle hierarchies altogether. 'God shows no partiality', he asserted. But he proclaimed a law of love rather than the end of slavery. He wasn't going to let the chaos of a class revolution get in the way of sharing the gospel.

But ever since, the question of what Christianity really means for economic relations has remained an open one. In the early decades, the church cowered under the shadow of persecution. When Nero was looking for a scapegoat after a destructive conflagration in Rome, he took vengeance on the Christians. It was only after the conversion of Emperor Constantine in the early fourth century that the upper classes started to embrace the church in earnest. But this created a paradox. Before Constantine, the Christians were the ones who, in spite of hardship and persecution, proclaimed equality and hope. After Constantine, Christians started to proclaim the support of the emperor as witness to the truth of their faith, and the radical edge of their message began to blur.

In these circumstances there began to be a new kind of Christianity. Influential individuals, raised in wealth and comfort, started to renounce the benefits of their inheritance and adopt the life of the poor – not from disaster and despair, but from choice and calling. One man stopped being a Roman soldier and adopted the life of a monk. Despite being as unkempt as a peasant, his charisma drew a host of wealthy people to leave their old life and take up shacks or dwell in caves above the River Loire. He turned the world upside down. He was the most talked-about man in France, or Gaul as it was known. What was fundamentally changing was that no longer did being a Christian mean displaying God's blessings by enjoying wealth and splendour. That was not now the face of God for us to worship. Instead, imitating the Christ that went to the cross, the life of the disciple was to be one of chastity and self-denial. In 371 the people of the nearby city came to fetch him to be their bishop. They didn't want a bishop who imitated the Roman governors of the day, with palaces and grandeur. They wanted a bishop who showed them the Christ who went to the cross. He hid in a barn to avoid being taken from his monastic life. But he was betrayed by the honking of a gaggle of geese. From then on he was known by the name by which we know him today: Martin of Tours.

People told many stories about St Martin, but one above all: that when he'd been a soldier he'd encountered a shivering beggar at the gate of Amiens; and to clothe the man he had sliced his military cloak in two, keeping half for himself; that night he saw in a dream that the beggar was Christ. Roman convention expected benefactors to support the unfortunate of their own city. But Martin was from Hungary, not from Amiens: he was changing the rules, right there and then. Christians were to have no constraints on their range of obligation, nor any limit on the extent of their mercy. They were to love as broadly as God loves us in Christ.

It was a moral revolution for the church; a revolution Christians still struggle to comprehend and inhabit to this day. But on Good Friday, we're not so interested in the moral revolution as the theological one. And that theological question is highlighted by the hymn of Philippians 2. Christ emptied himself, taking the form of a slave, and humbled himself to the point of death on a cross. Therefore God also highly exalted him, that every tongue should confess that he is Lord. Here's the question. Is Jesus really naked, bruised, broken, and humble? Is God truly a beaten, battered, shattered slave? Or is this just something Jesus went through in order to encounter the worst of the human condition, and thus take every one of us up into God's divinity?

You can see the problems with both approaches. If we say Jesus becoming poor was just a device, it seems like it wasn't true to the heart of God, and that some kind of technique was used to satisfy God and prove God's commitment to us. Yet if we say Christ is truly a slave, that seems to valorize oppression and portray eternal life as anything but free and fruitful.

I want to go back to the point I made in chapter 9. We need to let go of the idea that God is simply good and we are simply bad and Good Friday is about an almighty gesture from one man that takes the obstacle away so God can finally forgive us. Instead what we're seeing today is that God's love towards us, God's desire for us, God's longing to be with us, make God naked, render God practically enslaved, reveal God's humility, simplicity and vulnerability.

If we assume God is activating some mechanism by which Jesus' death sets us all free, then God is our benefactor, not fundamentally changed by the process but releasing us from sin and death as a surgeon extracts a tumour from a body. But the cross shows us more than that. God isn't a busy deity, taking a break from constructing Milky Ways and filling black holes in order to set us free for everlasting life. God is utterly consumed by the longing to be with us and dwell eternally with us in Christ. God has no other plans. We are God's desire. Jesus is God's heart walking around in front of us. Jesus isn't an ambassador from head office. He's God in flesh and blood. Salvation isn't a patronizing benefit God bestows on the worthy. It's the bet on which God's whole life is staked. God in Christ is a slave because God is wholly owned by one desire above all else: to be our companion. The cross shows us that this desire costs God everything. God isn't weak and vulnerable in the sense that divinity was never up to that much anyway; God is weak and vulnerable because in Jesus we've seen what it is that means everything to God. We know God's secret. That makes God naked before us.

If Martin had remained powerful and influential, he'd have been imitating a God who's our benefactor, taking the trouble to give us salvation the way a wealthy Roman citizen would build a circus to entertain the popular classes. Only by divesting himself of comfort and privilege could Martin show that he loved God just as God loved him – nakedly, vulnerably, wholly, totally, truly. Christianity is indeed an ethic, by which the lucky share their goods with the unfortunate, class barriers are dismantled, and all find freedom in Christ's service. But more importantly it's a theology that's revealed on Good Friday: God is not distant, benevolent, but unruffled; God is utterly devoted to being with us, so much so that in Christ God becomes naked, vulnerable and transparent to the point of agonizing suffering.

One has to wonder whether all the elaborate atonement theories are a complicated way of avoiding the simple truth: that God is naked before us, longing for us to be truly loving, tender and uninhibited in return. That was all it was ever about.

II

Foolishness: The Proof of Love

For the message about the cross is foolishness to those who are perishing, but to us who are being saved it is the power of God. For it is written, 'I will destroy the wisdom of the wise, and the discernment of the discerning I will thwart.' Where is the one who is wise? Where is the scribe? Where is the debater of this age? Has not God made foolish the wisdom of the world? For since, in the wisdom of God, the world did not know God through wisdom, God decided, through the foolishness of our proclamation, to save those who believe. For Jews demand signs and Greeks desire wisdom, but we proclaim Christ crucified, a stumbling block to Jews and foolishness to Gentiles, but to those who are the called, both Jews and Greeks, Christ the power of God and the wisdom of God. For God's foolishness is wiser than human wisdom, and God's weakness is stronger than human strength. (1 Corinthians 1.18–25)

As a pastor I'm always alert to euphemisms, because when a person uses a euphemism it's an indication they're somehow out of their depth. They're in territory their hearts feel unready and their souls feel uncomfortable to explore. Consider these expressions. 'Couple of sandwiches short of a picnic.' 'Doesn't have both oars in the water.' 'Elevator's stuck between the floors.' 'Lights are on but nobody's home.' 'Not dealing from a full deck.' 'Wheels're spinning, but the hamster's long gone.' 'As the Australians say, "Couple of kangaroos short of a full paddock."'

All these expressions tread a line between saying someone's stupid, and saying they're mad. We talk a lot about celebrating diversity, and that means a deeper understanding of mental illness and a deeper respect for those of low IQ. But these expressions and a thousand like them aren't about misunderstanding mental illness or demeaning someone with low IQ. They hint at something beyond medical and psychological diagnosis. They're about someone we think is crazy, mad, so eccentric that we reach for a new metaphor. Someone who's done what no one in their right mind would ever do. Something that unsettles us deeply. Something that beggars belief.

Such a thing was the claim by the early Christians that they worshipped the crucified one. The Roman Empire was built on slavery. Slavery was a system of institutionalized terror. Those who made trouble were nailed naked to wooden crosses, to die a slow death, unable to prevent the ravenous birds pecking at their still-breathing midriff. They were a public example, sometimes lining the roads like a boulevard en route to the city that had dared to rebel. It was such an ignominious end that few ancient authors lowered themselves to write about it.

To understand the gospel accounts of Jesus' crucifixion it's important to realize that what seems extraordinary to us isn't the same as what seemed noteworthy to people in the first century. Romans weren't scared off by the language of divinity. The son of God was a common title for the Emperor, and stories of people becoming gods were part of folklore. What the Romans simply couldn't comprehend was the veneration of a crucified man. Heroes crucified others: they weren't tortured and humiliated themselves. The Jews found it even harder. For them, there was only one God, who was Lord over all other powers in the heavens. That God held heaven and earth in glorious array. The idea that such a God could have an earthly son, and that that son could have been executed like a quarrelsome slave, was horrifying and absurd. Anyone who suggested such a thing must be out of their mind.

It's often said that portrayals of the cross in visual and artistic form don't appear until about 400 years after Jesus' death. That's because it was simply such an indescribable event, such a profound paradox, that the high and mighty one should die in such agonized ignominy. It's only after this period, after a time when the actual use of crucifixion as a form of torture, punishment, intimidation and social control had long passed, that theologians started to elaborate understandings of the cross that made it part of some forensic, mathematical or precise divine plan. The earliest atonement theories focused on the wonder of Jesus' resurrection – the only way they could talk about the cross was to see it as some kind of tactical defeat that preceded God's inevitable victory. But in the Middle Ages theories appeared that began to speak of the cross as some kind of adequate atonement for human sin, or some kind of due paid to a God who had to respect an honour code.

In one of the earliest Christian documents Paul seems to problematize any such tidy account of the cross. Jesus' crucifixion is utter foolishness in the culture of his time. To suggest any meaning or design could be found in it was nonsensical. Which is why it's so important today to recognize not just the indescribable pain of crucifixion, but the utter social disgrace and unutterable shame incurred. This cannot be part of some organized plan. It can only be an utter catastrophe.

The desire to make the cross part of some foreordained plan is an entirely understandable reaction in the face of horror and chaos. Life is full of fragility and danger. Suffering and pain are never far away. To see Christ as entering into that realm of terror, jumping into the raging torrent with no ability to reach the bank, is like realizing the universe is spiralling out of control and no one's in charge. It's absurd to deny that this is a terrifying prospect. But unless we name this horror, and feel the shiver of God being out of control, we're not truly entering the depth of what the cross demands of us. How can we shrug our shoulders and come to terms with the cross, feel secure in knowing it was all preordained, resolve to keep calm and carry on? God names all our hope that there is truth, beauty and goodness at the epicentre of all things, and the cross names our panic that this truth, beauty and goodness has lost control of events.

How can this be? What is the one force that has the capacity to reduce the most dominant character to powerlessness and the most terrifying power to trembling vulnerability? Love. There's only one reason why Jesus goes to the cross. It's not a grotesquely blundering coup d'état, or a naïve and hapless revolution. It's an empty-handed journey across the mystery of time to win our hearts to the cause of love. It's a completely crazy thing to do.

1700 years ago in the Egyptian desert there lived St Antony. He was the first Christian monk. This is how he described his life. 'A time is coming', he said, 'when everyone will go mad. And when they meet someone who's not mad, they'll say, "You are mad: you are not like us."' That time had already come. Everyone went mad, and they met the one person who was not mad, and they said, 'You are mad: you are not like us.' The one they met was Jesus. 'Wheels're spinning, but the hamster's long gone', they said. And we've said the same thing, but in a different way. They couldn't work out how God could be emptied of all but love. We can't conceive of how God could love so much as to risk Christ's cross. But who's crazy? And who's wise?

Rohinton Mistry's 1995 novel *A Fine Balance* is an account of life in India under the 1975 Emergency. The novel describes the fine balance between hope and despair, between the paradox of poverty and the initiative of survival, between the colour of life and the drabness of suffering. In the midst of the novel surfaces a unique character. Shankar is a man without legs or fingers, and is hence known by many as Worm. He shuffles and manoeuvres about on what he calls a gaadi, but we might imagine as some kind of skateboard. Shankar has a remarkable lack of self-pity and a generally sunny disposition. He lives under the sway of his pimp, whom he knows as Beggarmaster. Surprisingly Shankar sees Beggarmaster not as a figure of manipulation and oppression, but as a man of virtue to which he professes unending gratitude. In a typical scene, Shankar matter-of-factly explains his uncomplicated and uncomplaining view of the universe. He and others are discussing why they've been rounded up and taken to a site of slave labour. 'That's what I cannot understand', says Shankar. 'Why did police take me? Beggarmaster pays them every week – all his beggars are allowed to work without harassment.' The neighbours speculate that maybe these police don't know Beggarmaster. Shankar shakes his head at the absurdity of the suggestion. 'Everybody knows Beggarmaster', he says, conclusively. When the tailors enquire what happened to his legs and hands, Shankar is philosophical. 'Don't know, exactly. Always been like this. But I'm not complaining. I get enough to eat, plus a reserved place on the pavement. Beggarmaster looks after everything.' He becomes nostalgic, remembering the time before he had his gaadi, when he used to be carried around. 'Beggarmaster used to rent me out each day', he recalls. 'He would say I earned him the highest profits.'

Shankar seems like a fool. He looks like he's being duped by his pimp, exploited by those around him and despised by the harsh world. But though he experiences multiple hardships, he turns them not into bitterness or resentment but into compassion, kindness and playfulness. Rohinton Mistry trains the reader's moral compass by showing the texture and complexity of the human heart and conscience. Shankar comes to resemble India itself – beleaguered by suffering and tragedy, yet consistently resilient and resourceful in ways that transcend sympathy.

Mistry trains us through the figure of the legless, fingerless Shankar, to appreciate the foolishness of God. The cross is not part of a tidy plan. It's the foolishness of the dignity of love.

12

Example: Displaying God's Purpose

For to this you have been called, because Christ also suffered for you, leaving you an example, so that you should follow in his steps. 'He committed no sin, and no deceit was found in his mouth.' When he was abused, he did not return abuse; when he suffered, he did not threaten; but he entrusted himself to the one who judges justly. He himself bore our sins in his body on the cross, so that, free from sins, we might live for righteousness; by his wounds you have been healed. (1 Peter 2.21–24)

In the great debates about the cross the battle lines are usually drawn between those who believe something really changes between God and us through Jesus' death, often known as an objective atonement, and those who believe what really changes is the human heart, which is moved by Christ's example – often known as subjective atonement. The first group are usually so furious that the second group are settling for second best that it can come as a surprise to find, here in First Peter, a clear endorsement of the second view, referring to Christ as an example for us to follow.

What really does change as a result of the cross? Can we sift through the centuries of reflection and theorizing and find an answer? We have to start by acknowledging problems with the conventional view. The conventional view says that there was a Fall, and in response, in the fullness of time, God sent Jesus, whose death brought salvation. That salvation, though unlimited in extent, being forever, was limited in scope, in that it achieved heavenly bliss but left earthly existence unchanged.

There's two major problems with this view. The first is that only some seem to be saved – which surely can't have been God's purpose. The second is that it encourages a profound complacency. Where does that put the Holocaust, the Asian Tsunami, and the present pandemic? Surely if Jesus changes everything we'd see that change here and now?

I believe the problem lies in the whole idea that Jesus came to fix the results of the Fall. Instead I believe Christ's incarnation was at the heart of God's purposes in creation – indeed it was the reason for creation – and is far from a secondary action of God in response to the setback of sin and death. The incarnation wasn't an afterthought. It was always in the DNA of creation. God's life was, from the outset, ordered to be in relationship with us. The gospel is not that God responded to our sin by diverting from other duties to fit in a sacrificial intervention on earth to justify and sanctify us; the gospel is that being with us is written into the nature of God, and Christ's coming fully embodied what was always God's purpose.

So what do we do with the fact that evil is still very much around, as much as ever? We can perceive a negative and a positive answer. The negative aspect is hard to say but important to recognize. Jesus' work on the cross did not destroy death, did not dismantle sin, did not dispel evil. It sounds heretical to say it; but the evidence is incontrovertible: people still die, people continue in sin, evil persists. Jesus certainly confirms that sin, death and evil do not have the last word. But they still seem pretty loquacious right now. All of which is no more than to say, in more precise theological terms, Jesus' first coming has the same character but different outcomes to his second coming. His second coming does bring death, sin and evil to an end. When we lament and rail at God, it's generally because we want Christ's first coming to be more like his second coming. But that's a desire to bring history to an end – its good features as well as its bad ones. One day that'll happen, but there'll be losses as well as gains, and we have to assume that from God's point of view right now those losses outweigh the gains.

So what was Jesus' achievement on the cross, if it didn't as yet destroy death, dismantle sin, or dispel evil? I suggest two things.

The first is that it disclosed the virulence yet ultimate failure of evil. It displayed God's faithfulness, the offer of forgiveness of sin and reconciliation with God, the overcoming of death and the gift of eternal life. The cross does not eradicate evil and sin, but it demonstrates their damage, breaks their hold on humankind, and anticipates their final and conclusive demise.

The second thing I suggest constitutes Christ's work on earth is to demonstrate in utter, unmistakeable and sacrificial terms that nothing can separate us from the love of God. In Romans 8 Paul lists 17 things that he is convinced cannot separate us from the love of God in Jesus Christ our Lord: hardship, distress, persecution, famine, nakedness, peril, sword, death, life, angels, rulers, things present, things to come, powers, height, depth, and anything else in all creation. This list broadly describes Christ's experience in going to the cross. In the cry of dereliction we see Christ's utter commitment to be with us, even if it jeopardizes his relationship with the Father; and at the same time we see the Father's utter commitment to let Jesus be with us, even if it jeopardizes the inner-trinitarian Father-Son relationship. On those two commitments rest our salvation. Evil is that which threatens to separate us from the love of God; sin is action that ignores, forgets, misrepresents or repudiates the love of God. Christ's work demonstrates that this separation is never total and will not be final. We were created to be with ourselves, one another, the creation and God forever; and God's will to make it so eternally shall not be thwarted.

My contention is that our understanding of the cross, like most of our theology, has become captivated by the notion of for, to the detriment of the truer reality of with. By this I mean that we invariably perceive Christ as working for us – fixing our infirmities, dying for us, rising for us – rather than focusing on the more lasting gift of his working with or ultimately being with us. On the last day, as Revelation 21 tells us, God will be with us. In the coming of the kingdom, once the tears have been wiped away, there'll be nothing left for God to do for us. We shall fully be God's companions. The relationship will be the utter embodiment of with. What I'm suggesting is that with is not only the *goal* of salvation; it's also the *method* of salvation. God is with us through the very worst of life and in the very separation of death – in, through, and beyond. Jesus isn't spared the cross. Jesus isn't rescued from the cross. Jesus is with God on the cross. The bonds of the Trinity are stretched to the limit; but not broken. When we see the cross we see that God is with us, however, whatever, wherever ... forever. This is our faith.

You may know Elie Wiesel's much-quoted account in his book *Night* of the hanging of two men and a child in Auschwitz. These are Wiesel's powerful words.

The two men were no longer alive. Their tongues were hanging out, swollen and bluish. But the third rope was still moving: the child, too light, was still breathing ...

And so he remained for more than half an hour, lingering between life and death, writhing before our eyes. And we were forced to look at him at close range. He was still alive when I passed him. His tongue was still red, his eyes not yet extinguished.

Behind me, I heard [a] man asking: 'For God's sake, where is God?' And from within me, I heard a voice answer: 'Where is He? This is where – hanging here from this gallows ...'

The paradox of this story is that it narrates Wiesel's own loss of faith in what I call the 'God of for' – while at the same time poignantly affirming both the identity and method of what I call the 'God of with.' For a theology of 'for', this is the death of a powerless God who's incapable of sustaining sovereign authority in the face of overwhelming evil. For a theology of 'with', this is a Christlike moment of utter solidarity with the oppressed of the earth – a moment when humanity shares in the humanity of God. It's an iconic instant that demonstrates how evil hurts God at least as much as it damages victims or disgraces humankind.

Which is why we need to rehabilitate the idea of Jesus' cross as an example. It's not a soft atonement, unable to do the objective work of defeating death. Jesus' work on earth was not straightaway to destroy death, dismantle sin, or dispel evil; neither was it to rescue souls for heavenly bliss that they might temporally escape bleak earth and eternally evade excruciating hell. It was to display the purpose of God ultimately to bring a kingdom beyond death, sin and evil, and to demonstrate conclusively the original design of God to be with us always, most especially in our moments of distress and isolation. Jesus ascended into heaven when in his resurrection he had demonstrated the promise of the kingdom, and in his crucifixion he had shown the will never to be separated from us.

The cross doesn't make everything perfect straightaway. But we put it in our churches and on our walls and around our necks to say, 'The God who will go to that length to be with us, will, I believe, be with us always.'

13

Reconciliation: The Breaking Point

For he is our peace; in his flesh he has made both groups into one and has broken down the dividing wall, that is, the hostility between us. He has abolished the law with its commandments and ordinances, that he might create in himself one new humanity in place of the two, thus making peace, and might reconcile both groups to God in one body through the cross, thus putting to death that hostility through it. So he came and proclaimed peace to you who were far off and peace to those who were near; for through him both of us have access in one Spirit to the Father. So then you are no longer strangers and aliens, but you are citizens with the saints and also members of the household of God, built upon the foundation of the apostles and prophets, with Christ Jesus himself as the cornerstone. (Ephesians 2.14–20)

Not long ago I learned about what it's like to be a newly qualified nurse on many NHS wards. I heard about a woman whose children were at an age when many parents feel torn between the responsibilities of work and the duties of home. Nonetheless she embarked on training to be a nurse. She struggled to face the challenge of understaffing while herself experiencing new emotional thresholds like seeing a dead body for the first time. She frequently found herself distributing medications at a time of day when there weren't sufficient colleagues on the ward, and knew she had made mistakes. She was on a ward where profoundly mentally ill patients, some of whom could be violent, were being cared for alongside terminally ill patients receiving palliative care. Physical danger from the one was daily balanced against heartbreak from the other. Nurses were permitted to work 37 regular hours a week and up to 40 bank hours. She felt guilty if she didn't do a lot of bank hours but she was physically and mentally exhausted. It wasn't enough simply to train more staff because each ward needed a balance of skilled and trainee nurses. She felt like the strains on the NHS were coruscating through her own body. She was passionate about her work, but she got to the stage where she was near collapse and the effects were being felt within her family. She'd reached breaking point.

Breaking point. It's the moment where conflicting demands pull you in different directions and you can no longer keep all your commitments. In medieval France, a hideous form of death by torture was devised known as quartering. A rope was attached to each of the victim's four limbs. These ropes were each fastened to four bars. Then a horse was harnessed to each bar, before the four horses, suitably whipped, careered off in different directions, straining each of the victim's limbs to breaking point at the same time.

It's an unspeakable physical torture. But it's comparable to the kind of struggle children go through when they find their two parents are so intent on fighting each other, everything else becomes a weapon or collateral damage. I once knew a child who talked me through her family tree. 'I've got my mum and my stepdad, my dad and my stepmum, my granny who's my mum's mum and my stepgrandad, my grandad who's my mum's dad and my step-granny, my gran who's my dad's mum and my step-grandad, my grandad who's my dad's dad and my step-gran. But my brother's actually my half-brother and he's got all the same as me, but half of his aren't the same as half of mine.' She was about twelve years old. I had no idea what more complications lay ahead of her. She hadn't even started on her uncles and aunts. But she hadn't finished. 'It's really horrible when I'm in the house and my mum and my step-dad are fighting, and he's saying she always puts me first, and she's saying,

"Are you asking me to choose between you and the children – because I'll always choose the children"; and then they both look at me and I feel my stepdad's envious of me because of what my mum's just said, and my mum's using me as a way to get what she wants when really she's just being mean to my stepdad. Sometimes I just go to my bedroom and cry because I think if I wasn't here it would be easier for everyone. But then I realize if I wasn't here they'd just find something else to hit each other with – and that makes me feel worse because I feel like I'm just a weapon and good for nothing else.' How many children today could tell a story just like that?

Consider these mysterious words from Ephesians. 'In his flesh he has made both groups into one … that he might create in himself one new humanity in place of the two, thus making peace, and might reconcile both groups to God in one body through the cross, thus putting to death that hostility through it.' I want to reflect on these three powerful images I've been sharing. In the first, a nurse reaches breaking point, feeling in her own body the conflicting demands of professional duty, personal vocation and family responsibility amid a backdrop of understaffing and closed psychiatric wards. In the second, a medieval torture victim literally feels his body reaching breaking point, quartered by being pulled like a barge in four directions. In the third, a child becomes the battleground for a host of broken family relationships.

What these three images and the words from Ephesians add up to is this. Jesus on the cross is stretched to breaking point. He's fully human, and fully divine. He's at the point in history when those two identities are almost entirely incompatible, because in refusing to listen to him, humanity has rejected its calling to be the image of God in the world. The four horsemen of the apocalypse – pestilence, war, famine and death – those things that create such suffering in the world and question God's sovereignty; like an elaborate medieval torture, these four forces rack Christ's body in agony. As well as being the embodiment of the tension between humanity and God, and between suffering and providence, Christ crucified is, as Ephesians is most eager to point out, the place where the division between Jew and Gentile is played out. This is the moment, according to Ephesians, when Christ is the representative both of humanity and of Israel – the new Adam and the new Abraham.

We often concentrate on the physical anguish of the cross, but perhaps the heart of the cross is this sense of a breaking point between equal loyalties. The heart of our faith is that, when Christ was breaking apart in agony, he never let go of us. Which tells us that, in the heat of our agony, God will never let go of us. Even if it makes God the victim of a medieval torture of being pulled in every direction.

In 1998 a Frenchwoman called Denise Némirovsky deciphered a notebook in which, in microscopic handwriting, her mother Irène had written an account of life in rural France in the weeks following the fall of Paris in 1940. The book, and now film, known as *Suite Française*, tells the story of Lucile, whose unfaithful husband is a prisoner of war, and who lives with her mother-in-law in uncomfortable silences. When the Germans arrive, their commander, Bruno, is billeted with them in their house. Bruno turns out to be a talented pianist, and repeatedly plays the same composition, apparently his own, entitled 'Suite Française'. Lucile and Bruno fall in love. Bruno is privately unconvinced of the worthiness of the Nazi cause, and Lucile easily persuades him to do favours that, without his knowledge, enable her to shield a resistance fighter. Eventually Lucile extracts a pass to enable her to drive the resistance fighter to Paris. Bruno appears at just the moment the resistance fighter has killed two German guards. In this extraordinary scene, the three main characters face each other, all three both guilty and innocent. Lucile is torn between her love for Bruno and her loyalty to France and the resistance, Bruno is torn between his duty as a soldier and his love for Lucile, and the resistance fighter is torn between his commitment to armed struggle and his gratitude to Lucile. It's a breaking point for all three characters. The story's saying, this is life – if you love, if you try to keep commitments, if you seek to be a person of honour, if you stand for truth, life will bring you moments that are breaking points – moments when your body is a battleground for competing loyalties and conflicting duties.

It turns out reconciliation isn't a fantasy of beautiful relationships enjoyed on a cloud of harp music and tearful reunions. Reconciliation is right here: holding together profound but incompatible loyalties, straddling deep but rival relationships, being the battleground for terrible and uncontrollable enmities. We experience it on a human scale. Christ on the cross experiences it on a cosmic scale. It's the breaking point. It's the agony and glory of our salvation.

14

Boast: The Dirty Work

May I never boast of anything except the cross of our Lord Jesus Christ, by which the world has been crucified to me, and I to the world. For neither circumcision nor uncircumcision is anything; but a new creation is everything! As for those who will follow this rule – peace be upon them, and mercy, and upon the Israel of God. (Galatians 6.14–16)

In the crucified Jesus, we hear God saying, 'I wear my heart on my sleeve.' Jesus' cross isn't that complicated: it's God saying, 'This is how much I love you.' It's a judgement on every other inadequate gesture of love.

We all make judgements, even if we pretend we don't. This time of pandemic has been one of incessant judgements – who's not observing distancing guidelines, who's gone for too much exercise today, who should have taken a bigger pay cut. Judgement is everywhere. A few months ago, one person made a very severe judgement on me. I received a letter from a woman I haven't met, but who is nonetheless convinced of all my faults – and more. She believed everything she read in the newspaper about the death of a young homeless man on the streets of London, and wrote to tell me how outraged she was.

My chief sin, it turns out, is not to be one particular predecessor. 'It could not have happened in his time', the letter asserted. 'You have turned that lovely, caring community run by lovely gentle gentlemen in my time, into a modern-day business, bent on efficiency.' It seems the glorious amateurs have been replaced by hard-nosed professionals – myself chief among them. 'When I think of the saints who worked there, I could weep.' The rhetorical dial went up a couple of notches. But she hadn't finished. 'Shame on you.' And then the peroration: 'Don't sleep easy in your bed tonight. And tomorrow roll up your sleeves and do some of the dirty work.'

She didn't explain precisely what the dirty work was. It took me back to a rather conflictual relationship many years ago, when my parishioner detonated a nuclear judgement: 'You have failed this community as a priest.' No answer to that. The scar abides.

I got an insight into the dirty work later the same day. I put the letter to one side, on hand to burst the balloon should my ego ever inflate to dangerous levels. But then I received a message from a person whom a few years ago I got to know very well, in a way only a pastor really can. He was experiencing about the worst thing a person can ever go through. His child, young and full of life, had injected a recreational drug that turned out to have been contaminated. She went into a coma, and never emerged; she died a month later. He'd asked me to take her funeral. It was one of the toughest challenges I've ever had.

What do you say in the face of such indescribable tragedy? A lively young person dying an absurd and pointless death, shrouded in grief, horror and shame. It seemed her father had felt I'd got something right, because, the same evening I'd got the poison-ink letter, I was on the phone to him, and he was asking me to take his brother's funeral. I live my life by appointments and schedules, so fitting in a funeral was no simple matter: but sometimes you simply eradicate 'No' from your vocabulary.

This gentle man, for whom losing a brother compounded the loss of his vivacious daughter, then sent me one of the most extraordinary messages I've ever received. He reminded me that at his daughter's service I'd preached from the Song of Songs. I'd read the words, 'Set me as a seal upon your heart, a seal upon your arm; for love is strong as death.' This is what I'd said. 'The whole Bible is in this sentence; the Christian faith rests on the belief that love is stronger than death: and Christian hope is simply this – that we are a seal upon God's heart.'

It was starting to come back to me now. But his gentle message went on, 'At her funeral, my son was so upset that I wondered whether he'd taken much of it in. For the rest of that summer he withdrew from us and from most people. Some weeks later he acquired, on the inside of his right forearm, an indecipherable tattoo. It turned out that he'd asked my wife, in her beautiful handwriting, to write eight short words, which he'd then had permanently tattooed in mirror image. He decided on mirror image, he said, "Because I don't want people knowing my business." The eight words were, "Set me as a seal upon your heart." The tattoo looks like a blur in ordinary sight. The words emerge for my son when he holds his arm up before a mirror. (And of course the verse continues: ... "as a seal upon your arm").'

I didn't know what to say; how to reply. How can we ever know what people are really thinking after so tragically losing a loved one, since we so seldom ask them to roll up their sleeves and provide the evidence? But what I do know is this. Christ rolls up his sleeves in ministry around Galilee. In Jerusalem he rolls up his sleeves and bares his arm and shows us that love is strong as death, passion as fierce as the grave; and tattooed on his arm is our name – my name, Sam, and your name, too: but the names look like a blur and are indecipherable, probably because he didn't want people knowing his business. And on the cross Christ sets us as a seal upon his heart, and we're sealed on that arm forever – you, me, that father, his two children, his wife, and his brother.

And the woman who wrote me the poisoned letter. Her name is written in the indecipherable tattoo on Christ's arm too. She wanted me to roll up my sleeves and do some of the dirty work. What the bereaved father's extraordinary message told me is that Christ has already rolled up his sleeves and done the dirty work. Any work I might do, clean or dirty, is simply a celebration of that.

Christ rolled up his sleeves, and did the dirty work. That's the cross. The dirty work was to seal us on his arm, and in God's heart, forever.

PART 4

The Cross in the Gospels

15

Finished

When Jesus knew that all was now finished, he said (in order
to fulfil the scripture), 'I am thirsty.' A jar full of sour wine
was standing there. So they put a sponge full of the wine on
a branch of hyssop and held it to his mouth. When Jesus had
received the wine, he said, 'It is finished.' Then he bowed his
head and gave up his spirit. (John 19.28–30)

Here is a naked man. He's been beaten to pulp. He's bleeding
hand and foot. His arms are spreadeagled so he can't fight off
the flies or wipe away the sweat and the blood. He's practically
alone. He's more or less isolated. He's totally humiliated. It's
almost impossible to look at a picture of such agony and misery.

And at the climax of this ghastly scene, John's gospel tells us,
this man says one single word. 'Finished.' Finished. Think for
a moment about the host of meanings of that word. Finished.
The dissertation's finally edited and handed in. Finished. The
marathon's run and I'm totally done in. Finished. The relationship's over and she's told me she doesn't love me. Finished. The
work of art is completed and ready for display. Finished. The
counselling has run its course and I can face the world without
fear or bitterness or anger. Finished. I've served my sentence
and I can come out of prison. Finished. I've been told I've no
longer got a job and needn't come back to work. Finished.

Surely Jesus' climactic words from the cross must be ironic.
This isn't the way the story was supposed to end. Remember
the heavenly host of angels in the skies above Bethlehem
singing of peace on earth? Surely this wasn't the way they

imagined it would all turn out. Remember the crowds on Palm Sunday waving branches and shouting Hosanna? Surely they weren't thinking of this apocalypse five days later. A lot of other words might capture it. Ruined, betrayed, wasted, lost, destroyed, devastated, ravaged, spoiled, wrecked ... but not 'finished'. What might this word 'finished' mean? Let's look a little closer. Let's see if we can discover what is finished by Friday afternoon.

One thing that's finished is the blond Jesus with the constant smile, the loose-fitting toga and the baby lamb constantly around his neck like a primal life-jacket. That would be the Jesus whose picture perched above my bed as a child. The one that loves the little children. There's nothing sentimental about the cross. There's no guitar-playing, commune-dwelling, tie-dying, knitted-yogurt-eating, country-road-singing, long-haired-lover-from-Liverpool, John Denver-bespectacled Jesus in the face of Good Friday. Jesus is mutilated. He's taunted. He's asphyxiated. The Jesus of our projections, the kind friend, the handsome suitor, the Mr Fixit, the husky organic farmer, the country sage, the wandering minstrel – they all die at the foot of the cross. The rose-tinted Jesus of soft-focused promotional paraphernalia is gone. Finished.

Another thing that's finished is the conquering Jesus with the righteous fist, the Jesus whom the Crusader thought he was upholding as he smashed the head of the infidel, the Jesus whom the Inquisition thought it was promoting by torture and cruelty, the Jesus proclaimed by conquistadores with colonial mind-sets and rapacious ambitions, the Jesus that demands to seize control of the government, the Jesus that obliterates other religions from the face of the earth, the Jesus whose name is invoked to justify one race or people or gender giving themselves sanction to oppress and marginalize and lord it over others. On Good Friday Jesus doesn't conquer. He's humiliated. He's defeated. He's dragged through the streets like a slave or a dog. The Jesus that gives credibility to human power-grabs is gone. Finished.

And that's by no means all. The Jesus that makes for good citizenship and stable social relations is finished too. Jesus died a criminal's death. We can plead his innocence as long as we like, but in the eyes of the Sanhedrin he was acting as if he was the Messiah, the Son of God, the one who was bringing Israel's long exile to an end. And that meant he had to die. And in the eyes of the Romans he was a rabble-rouser and a potential king, and that made him guilty of a capital crime. Jesus was a good citizen of the kingdom of heaven, but not a very reliable citizen of Rome. So the meek Jesus that believes in law and order, the mild Jesus that instructs children to be good and kind and to obey their parents, the Jesus that doesn't want to rock the political boat or disturb the neighbours – that Jesus dies in the face of the cross. That Jesus is finished.

And what about the Jesus of a mathematical equation – the Jesus that says, 'Take one drop of total human depravity, add one pinch of utter divine grace, mix with one broken law and blend in one innocent death, and then subtract one angry devil'? That Jesus, who seems subject to some extraneous logic invisible to the eyes of the disciples but obvious to the well-informed cosmic legal historian, that Jesus disintegrates in the face of the circumstantial detail of the cross. If Jesus were simply a component in a mathematical equation or legal formula that got us off the devil's hook, then why would the gospels tell us so much about the disciples who deserted him, the women who followed him, the mother who loved him, the sinners he forgave, the sick he healed, the poor he accompanied, the blind he led? By the time we get to the cross the gospels have shown us enough about Jesus not just to show us how much he loves us but to make us love him. You don't love a formula or an equation. The cross shows us not forensic symmetry but wondrous love. The Jesus of the divine bargain is finished.

And then there's the Jesus that watches idly by while earthquakes destroy countries, while a pandemic afflicts a generation, while civil war becomes a way of life across the world, while loved ones develop cancer, while drought afflicts continents,

while hurricanes and tsunamis wreck households and liveli-
hoods and cities. Nero watched from afar and fiddled while
Rome burned; but Jesus isn't looking idly through some heavenly telescope. Jesus is suffering an agony as bad as any known
to human experience. Jesus isn't tucked up in the sky, peering
down from a safe distance: he's in the middle of a human train
crash, the glass and wheels and rails and twisted metal all con-
torting his body and piercing his soul. If you ever look up to
the sky and shout 'Oh God, why?' you're looking in the wrong
place. You need to be looking into the face of the crucified
Jesus. That distant remote-control God has got nothing to do
with Christianity. In the face of the cross, that Jesus is finished.

And here's a painful one. The Jesus that belongs to the
church, the Jesus that gives an affirming thumbs-up to everything
Christians set out to do, the Jesus that makes a congregation
a circle of holiness and a cradle of wholesomeness – that
Jesus withers in the face of the cross. It's not clear when the
church begins. Maybe when Jesus gives Peter the keys of the
kingdom. Maybe when Jesus says to Peter, 'Feed my Sheep.'
Maybe when Jesus breathes on the disciples and says, 'I send
you.' Maybe when the Holy Spirit comes down at Pentecost.
But a good candidate for the beginning of the church is right
here at the cross, when Jesus hands his mother over to the care
of the beloved disciple. You can see Mary representing Israel
and the beloved disciple representing the church, and Jesus'
instructions portraying the inextricable destiny of the two. Not
a glamorous scene, is it? This is two fragile figures amid a vista
of apocalyptic devastation. Not exactly a mega-church bent
on growth. Lends a whole new irony to Jesus' words, 'Where
two or three are gathered, I am with them', doesn't it? In the
face of the cross, there's no place for the self-congratulatory
church that's holier than God. There's only a place for church
that looks like Jesus. Any other church is like any other Jesus.
It's finished.

But here's the most important one of all. The cross confronts
us with the fragility of Jesus. He's no superman who leaps down

and says, 'Only joking!' He suffers to the end. We wonder how this awful spectacle can possibly be necessary for our salvation. We're supposed to wonder that. We wonder whether this tiny, broken, wasted body can possibly be the body of God. We're supposed to wonder that. We wonder how any joy, any hope, any glory can possibly emerge from this hideous catastrophe. We're supposed to wonder that. We wonder why God doesn't utterly reject us after we've shown the very worst that we can do. We're supposed to wonder that. All of those wonderings should be part of our faith, our imagination, our daily prayer and our compassionate hearts. But for all our wondering and pondering, one thing is utterly clear. When we see the pain, when we feel the grief, when we look upon the loneliness, when we touch the wounds, when we hear the cries, we know, we know that God will go to any lengths for us, God will never be separated from us, that loving us is written into God's DNA, that there's no part of God that has any desire to be except to be with us, that Jesus is the embodiment of the way God's destiny is wrapped up in us forever. Any other notion of God, any other speculation about God's wishes, any other idea about what lies at the heart of God is gone. Over. Dispelled. Finished.

Jesus' final word: 'finished'. His life is finished. His ministry's finished. The scriptures are finished. The reconciliation of God and creation is finished. And a host of misconceptions are dispatched at the same time. Jesus isn't a cosy companion. He's not a triumphalist conqueror. He's not a law-abiding do-gooder. He's not legal formula. He's not a heartless onlooker. He's not a pretext for Christian self-satisfaction. All those idolatries are finished. They're snuffed out like a line of candles, one by one. Finished. Finished. Finished. Finished. Finished. Finished. Finished.

Everything's finished. Everything's desolate. Everything's laid waste. Everything's lost, except the heart of God laid bare. And if we're not seduced by a comforting saviour, if we're not mesmerized by a merciless hero, if we're not domesticated by a model citizen, if we're not obsessed by a mathematical equation, if we're not alienated by a distant deity, if we haven't fled from the cross like most of the church for most of its history, we might just get close enough to glimpse that sacred heart laid bare. And we might just get to read what's written on that heart, pierced and finished from love of us. And we might just believe these words we see written there: 'I swear to you our time has just begun.'

16

Betrayed

When Judas, his betrayer, saw that Jesus was condemned, he repented and brought back the thirty pieces of silver to the chief priests and the elders. He said, 'I have sinned by betraying innocent blood.' But they said, 'What is that to us? See to it yourself.' Throwing down the pieces of silver in the temple, he departed; and he went and hanged himself. But the chief priests, taking the pieces of silver, said, 'It is not lawful to put them into the treasury, since they are blood money.' After conferring together, they used them to buy the potter's field as a place to bury foreigners. For this reason that field has been called the Field of Blood to this day. Then was fulfilled what had been spoken through the prophet Jeremiah, 'And they took the thirty pieces of silver, the price of the one on whom a price had been set, on whom some of the people of Israel had set a price, and they gave them for the potter's field, as the Lord commanded me.' (Matthew 27.3–10)

I was once involved in a production of twelve plays that portrayed the life of Jesus. All the plays were performed in a parish church. The play in which Jesus was betrayed by Judas took place at 10 o'clock at night on Maundy Thursday. When Judas realized what he'd done, and that the chief priests and the elders had turned their back on him, he started to tremble, and shake his head. He ran out of the church shouting 'Unclean ... unclean.' He ran down the road beside the church, all the way shouting 'Unclean ...', his distant cries echoing amid the stunned silence of the audience. I'll never forget that moment.

I want to reflect on Judas. I want to read his story three times – first as a story of one man's personal tragedy; again as a story of each one of us, at the foot of the cross; and third as a window into the whole work of God.

So let's start with Judas himself. What can he possibly have been thinking? Let's imagine Judas saw himself as a sharper and altogether more significant figure than the journeymen disciples. You can see him as the one always looking to theorize, to analyse, to generalize – reluctant to take Jesus at face value, always looking to see extra interests and manoeuvrings at work whenever Jesus was healing or teaching. We can picture Judas, slightly to one side of the crowds following Jesus, as if to say, 'I have other options, you know; I'm following Jesus because he draws a crowd, but Jesus may not end up being the best way of getting what Israel wants and needs – I'm reserving judgement on that.'

And yet Judas loves Jesus. He's moved by the parables, inspired by the walk to Jerusalem, awed by the healings; he can't deny that in Jesus he has truly seen the kingdom of God. He's almost embarrassed by his love for Jesus. In a previous post I was once visited by a senior city official who hadn't been to church for years, but secretly wrote praise songs. He came to my house one morning and left with me a CD of a song he'd just written. He handed it to me for safe keeping as furtively as if he were giving me a brown envelope of pornographic photographs. I imagine Judas like this city official – embarrassed that a man of his intelligence should secretly love Jesus as much as the crowds and the poor and the common people did. Judas can't bring himself to worship Jesus – he always wants Jesus to be a means to some greater end.

And you can sense a mounting frustration as he sees Jesus failing to take his many opportunities to seize power. The defining moment is the anointing at Bethany: Jesus lets the woman's devotion to him be utterly wasted by pouring perfume out in a symbolic act of burial, while Judas sees that such devotion should have been harnessed for a popular movement, such resources should have fed hungry mouths, and a symbolic burial is pious nonsense when there's a resistance movement to organize. Judas betrays Jesus out of impatience at his style of leadership, jealousy at his magnetic personality, and fury that he seems to be making beautiful gestures rather than seizing the initiative. Finally Judas resorts to a clumsy effort at provocation, and, in as many words, says to Jesus, 'If you're not going to do what I know is good for you, I'm going to trap you in a position where you have no alternative.'

And so Judas leads the chief priests' henchmen to Gethsemane, and kisses Jesus. The kiss is a gesture of self-hatred, if you imagine that Judas resents how much he loves Jesus. Judas is literally trying to turn his love for Jesus into something he regards as more important. He contrives to bring the most powerful forces in Israel together – the chief priests and Jesus. He assumes the priests' pragmatism and the messiah's passion will make an unstoppable combination. But in no time at all he realizes Jesus has been handed over to the Romans, which can only mean certain death, and all Judas has to show from the planning and scheming and devotion and analysis of three years on the road with Jesus, all he has left to bring about the kingdom of God single-handed, is thirty pieces of silver. Beside himself, he goes back to the chief priests and says, 'It wasn't supposed to turn out like this. I was supposed to be the hero.' But the priests just laugh, and say, 'You thought Jesus could be your tool. Turns out you were ours.' Not just his discipleship, but the whole life project of Judas, to manipulate others to some unspecified greater end, is in tatters. Everything Judas stood for is exposed to himself and others as empty and cruel. It's unbearable. He hangs himself.

We want Judas to be uniquely evil, because then we can know that we couldn't have betrayed Jesus. We want Judas to be a monster; because we don't want him to be too much like us. But what we've already discovered is that Judas is all too much like us. Let's tell his story again a second time, in such a way that makes clear why Jesus went to the cross, and how much Judas is like us.

There are many ways in which we put our lives in other people's hands. When you step on a plane you put your life in the pilot's hands. When you step in a friend's car your life is in your friend's hands. When you lie on the operating table, your life is in the surgeon's hands. When you say to someone, 'I love you', you're telling them that your life, or at least your heart, is in their hands. Half the time we crave this power and responsibility, half the time we want to live as if we didn't have it. We crave the sense that we can hold someone's life or destiny in our hands – a baby maybe, or a person we adore and desire who finally comes to return our passion, a person in authority perhaps who recognizes us and gives us power. These people make us feel we really matter, matter because we hold their life in our hands and they matter. But then suddenly we discover we don't know what to do with that power. We wanted the big job but we have no idea how to live into it. We wanted the warmth and pride of everyone's attention but we don't know what to do with the spotlight.

Be careful what you hope for. Judas wanted to 'make a difference'. He craved a life that mattered – a life that affected not just the destiny of Israel but the destiny of all humankind. And … he got one. He had his hands on Jesus' heart. And he didn't know what to do with it. When he got it wrong he went to see the chief priests and asked for another go. And they laughed at him. 'That's your problem,' they said. So finally he had only one thing left he could control – the nature and timing of his end. He was so set on his life mattering that he decided he alone could determine the meaning of his own death.

And this, I think, is what betrayal means. This is what took Jesus to the cross. It's when we don't believe our lives matter so we go looking for ways to *make* them matter. And we greedily draw other people into our net, one maybe, or several, or possibly a great many. Perhaps we start by simply wanting others to have a good opinion of us. But soon we don't just want their opinions, we want more. We can't cope with our own lives being out of control so we reassure ourselves by controlling other people's lives – emotionally, physically, sexually, professionally, subtly, clumsily, with coercion or manipulation, in public or in private, with charm or by force: and the moment they realize they've just been a pawn in our pathetic attempts to make our own lives secure, the moment they realize our real commitments lie not with them but only with ourselves, the moment they realize how much they had come to put their life in our hands, that's the moment they see us for what we are and use the word 'betrayal'.

Treason (or spying) is often a betrayal because it shows you care more about yourself and your own ideas than you do about your country and its people. Breaking confidence is often a betrayal because it shows you don't value what someone else says to you until you can use it to amuse or impress a third party. Judas' kiss is an agonizing betrayal because his intimate gesture masks the fact that he regards friendship with God not as the ultimate privilege but as a mere means to a more important end. He can't imagine friendship with God is everything. And so he loses everything greedily looking for more.

Jesus seemed to have a different approach. He didn't draw others into his power. He gave his life into the hands of others. He loved his disciples, even Judas, and by loving them he gave them power over him. They could betray him, even to the point of death. One of them did. He began his life in human hands, the hands of Mary and Joseph. They had power over him. He'd been giving his life away since the very start. In Gethsemane he was given into the hands of those who were using Israel for their greater purposes. On the cross he literally gave his life away. The cross is the last word on our security systems, on our control-freakery, on our manipulation of others, on our drawing people into our own web of affirmation and gratification and attention-seeking. Jesus doesn't seize the initiative. Quite the opposite. Jesus saves us *by giving his life away.*

Judas can't grasp this. The moment he realizes he's become a pawn in someone else's game he commits suicide. For him, being under the control of people, especially people he now sees are empty, is the ultimate disaster. But for Jesus, life isn't a puppet show. He has no purpose beyond making, maintaining and restoring relationships. These relationships are not a means to something more important. They're all there is. For ever. Jesus is God becoming our companion and restoring the whole creation's companionship with God, for ever. Period. *There is no other motive.* We aren't pawns on God's chessboard. We're friends God's seeking to make. And the only way to be a friend is to give your life away. Not usually all at one go; but here God fundamentally, comprehensively, definitively *gives life away*, from no other motive other than to become friends with us and all creation for ever.

The result is that God is in our hands, as we recognize each time we receive the bread of Holy Communion. Because God is in our hands, we run the risk of betraying God every day. And we *do* betray God. We *do* treat God as a means to our own more important ends. We *do* make God into an instrument of our pathetic misguided attempts to find our own security by controlling others. *But God never betrays us.* God's life is fully handed over to us. God cannot betray us. It's impossible. It's unimaginable. It's not in God's nature. That's what the cross means.

And that brings us finally to Judas as a window into the whole work of God. When Judas returns the chief priests their thirty pieces of silver, there's a painfully ironic scene when these men who haven't hesitated to shed innocent blood are reluctant to hang onto the blood money. So they buy the potter's field as a place to bury foreigners. 'Potter's field.' In this phrase we hear two echoes of the prophet Jeremiah. First we remember Jeremiah's field, the one he bought just before the Babylonians invaded Jerusalem. We remember his unbelievable, prophetic gesture that said after a time in Exile the Jews would indeed return to Israel. And we sense that after a time in the exile of the tomb Jesus will indeed return to risen life. And second we remember Jeremiah's potter, the one whose pot was broken in his hands, who then fashioned a new pot from the clay. And we see that the clay of Jesus is about to be broken in our hands, but that God will refashion a risen Jesus out of this same clay. And we step back even further and see that the clay of Israel has been broken in God's hands, and that God refashions a new destiny for Israel out of the same clay. That's the story of Israel. That's the story of Jesus. That's the story of the Bible. That's the story of God.

And Judas, the man of all the apostles whose name bears the name of the nation, Judah, is at the heart of this story. Judas shows us that the worst possible thing we can do is only made possible because God's life has in Jesus been given away to us, because God's life has been placed in our hands. And even the worst possible thing we can do can still be drawn back into the story of God. In fact, without the worst possible thing we can do we would never have seen the heart of who God is. It took Judas' betrayal and Jesus' consequent crucifixion for us to see that in Jesus, God's life really had been given away. So Judas is a microcosm of the whole gospel. God calls us, trusts us with heart and life, and even when we betray, even when we crucify, even when we're a broken pot or in self-imposed exile, even when we shout 'Unclean ...' and our plans are in tatters, God finds a way of bringing even our worst betrayal back into the story, of making us part of this saving work, and, in giving life away, gives life to us for ever. That was the good news of the first apostles. That's the good news today.

The chief priests betray the betrayer Judas when they say to him, 'See to it yourself.' We too betray Jesus. But God never betrays us. God never says to us, 'See to it yourself.' That's what we learn from Judas' story. That's what we learn from the cross. Whatever it takes, whatever we've done, whatever it costs – God never has and never will say to us, 'See to it yourself.' It's never just our problem. It's always God's problem. That's the good news of the cross. God will never leave us alone.

17

Pierced

Since it was the day of Preparation, the Jews did not want the bodies left on the cross during the sabbath, especially because that sabbath was a day of great solemnity. So they asked Pilate to have the legs of the crucified men broken and the bodies removed. Then the soldiers came and broke the legs of the first and of the other who had been crucified with him. But when they came to Jesus and saw that he was already dead, they did not break his legs. Instead, one of the soldiers pierced his side with a spear, and at once blood and water came out. (He who saw this has testified so that you also may believe. His testimony is true, and he knows that he tells the truth.) These things occurred so that the scripture might be fulfilled, 'None of his bones shall be broken.' And again another passage of scripture says, 'They will look on the one whom they have pierced.' (John 19.31–37)

One of the most privileged and tender moments you get invited into as a priest is to be with a person and their family at the moment of death. What I try to do is to touch the person's five senses and gently offer each one back to God. I touch their eyes and think about what those eyes have seen, their ears and reflect on what those ears have heard, their nose and savour what that nose has smelled, their mouth and dwell on what their tongue has tasted, and finally their hand and consider what their hands have touched.

I wonder if you've ever touched the skin of a person's body after they've died. It's an awesome and intimate thing to do.

It's terrifying, because it makes you realize how vulnerable each one of us is, because this moment will come for us all. But it also makes you ponder the intricate wonder of this person, how all the capillaries and nerve ends and organs and brain cells that are now silent and still were once so busy and creative for so long. Our physical bodies depend on two things above all. One is water – for we're each made up of about 60% water. The other is blood – for without the blood running around our bodies, nothing would function for more than a second.

Jesus has no nursing home or hospital side ward to die in. His execution is an extended and merciless form of relentless torture. Once Jesus has died, John's Gospel records a significant event. It says, 'One of the soldiers pierced his side with a spear, and at once blood and water came out.' It's an awesome event, of atonement and salvation, judgement, death and sacrifice, but it's also an intimate story of love and betrayal, physical pain and emotional heartbreak. What's going on throughout the passion narrative is an interweaving of awe and intimacy, of the grand cosmic story and the intense personal drama. I want to look at how all these things appear in this brutal moment shortly after Jesus' death, when the spear pierces his side and out come blood and water.

The first strand to weave is the background of this spear story in the ritual shape of Israel's life. The Day of Preparation falls every Friday, and ends at sundown on Friday night. Passover falls once a year, on the fourteenth day of the seventh month of the Jewish calendar, which can be any day of the week. John's Gospel points out that the day Jesus was killed was an unusual day, because the way the calendar fell it was *both* the eve of Passover *and* the Day of Preparation, a coincidence that only occurred every ten years or so. The fact that it was the eve of Passover meant that the blood that appeared as the soldier pierced Jesus side gushed forth just as the blood of the Passover lambs was being spilt. The fact that it was the Day of Preparation meant that those who had condemned Jesus wanted his body removed before the day of rest began. And all of this is told with repeated reminders that those who wanted Jesus dead could do nothing without the Romans' authority. Even the final spear thrust into Jesus' side is carried out by a Roman soldier. So already we have the grand context of sacrifice and deliverance and the earthier context of meeting legal requirements and avoiding the 24-hour sight and smell of a crucified corpse. But all of these are focused in the reality of a Roman soldier who has control over Jesus' body as surely as Rome had complete control over the land of Israel. Already we have themes of politics, personal passion and providential purpose all converging at this moment.

And then the next strand to weave is the resonance of these events in Israel's scriptures. Most obviously we recall the words concerning the suffering servant in Isaiah chapter 53 – 'He was pierced for our transgressions, crushed for our iniquities; ... and by his wounds we are healed.' But more subtly we might reflect on the Greek word for 'side', which is sometimes translated 'rib'. It appears only here in the New Testament and only once in the Greek version of the Old Testament. But that single place is very interesting. It's the moment in Genesis chapter 2 where God takes the side (or rib) of Adam and shapes it into a woman. The creation of Eve in Genesis chapter 2 represents not just the creation of woman, but the creation of society, of diversity, of the whole idea that human beings can share and give and pass on life to one another. So what we've got in this piercing of Jesus' side with the spear is not just the fulfilment the prophecy of the suffering servant, but also an idea that what comes out of Jesus may be the beginning of new life, a new society. When we recall Jesus' promise that from him will come streams of living water we begin to wonder if this is precisely what he was referring to.

And this invites the weaving of another strand, which we might call the significance of these events in the life of the church. What exactly is the meaning for the church of the account that out of Jesus at his death came water and blood?

Water and blood ... It's hard to avoid the most obvious connection of this event to the two central acts of the church's life:
baptism and Eucharist. We've already seen that this moment
on the cross is like Eve emerging out from the side of Adam,
like a new birth – almost a new creation. Now it seems like this
is like the birth of the church at the moment of Christ's death –
and in its birth it's given the two sacraments that shape its life,
the water of baptism and the blood of holy communion. Just
a few verses earlier Jesus has commended his mother to the
beloved disciple and the beloved disciple to his mother with the
words, 'Woman, here is your son', and, 'Here is your mother.'
So here at the cross we're witnessing the foundation of the
church, with a new community, a new birth and new sources
of life.

And that brings us finally to the last strand in understanding
what the piercing of Jesus' side and the blood and water are all
about. I've talked a bit about blood and I've talked a bit about
water. I want to talk a little about the word 'and'. John's quite
fond of the word 'and'. In John chapter one we get word *and*
flesh, grace *and* truth. In John chapter two we get water *and*
wine. In John chapter three we get spirit *and* truth. Later we
get resurrection *and* life. You get the idea. Here we get 'blood
and water'.

I believe that 'and' is the clue to how we're to interpret
Jesus' life and how to interpret Jesus' death. Remember what
I said about what it's like to touch a dead body. You get the
delicate intimacy of realizing you are close to the vulnerability
and fragility of another human being, maybe one you deeply
loved. But you also get the shiver of awe that this is death,
cold, numbing, unavoidable death, and it's as scary close up in
flesh and blood as it is far away in the language of oblivion and
judgement. Well I think we can take these twin feelings to this
moment of the death of Jesus. There's water – there's the way
Jesus' death gives life, gives hope, gives trust in the promises of
God and the presence of the Holy Spirit. And yet there's also
blood – there's pain, and horror, and brutality, and ugliness,

and violence and deep, deep fear. And John's account says, '*at once* blood and water came out'. In other words they came out together. The cross is about water *and* blood.

And the same is true if we look back at Jesus' life through the lens of his cross. There's water – there's fountains of life, living water, healing, forgiveness, joy and gladness. But there's also blood – there's hostility, betrayal, hatred, pain, adversity, and finally what looks very much like defeat. On Good Friday it's easy to make one of two mistakes – to look just on the watery Jesus, who saved us from our sins and made everything right between us and God, or to look just on the bloody Jesus, who suffered in agony and at the last believed God had forsaken him. That's why the *and* is so important.

Which is why the last strand in understanding the water and the blood of Jesus' pierced side is the kind of life you and I are to live in faithfulness to the moment of Jesus' death. We could live a life that airbrushes out the blood, and just sees the water – a sunny life that insists everything always turns out for the best, that won't tolerate gloom in ourselves and chases it out of everyone else, that fits the Jesus story into a positive and upbeat outlook on the world. Or we could live a life that airbrushes out the water, and just sees the blood – a life of struggle, and anger, and bitterness and a recognition that there really is hatred and enmity in the world and death comes to us all. But to follow the saviour from whose side at once came water *and* blood is to believe *both* that suffering and death are real *and* that Jesus' death and resurrection have transformed suffering and death so that they no longer have the last word. Because of the blood, what we see taking the place on the cross is terrifying: it's real human death. But because of the water, we can look upon it with hope, and not have to turn away our eyes in fear and despair. It's not the end of the story.

And so now that we've learned how to look at the glory and horror of the cross, look with me at the most agonizing sight in your own life. Look with me at what you've brought about by your own foolishness, at what you can't put right for all your attempts to ignore it or deny it or distract from it or resolve it. Dare to look with me at what you dare not look at very often, the truth about yourself, your life, your love, your fear, your faith. And look with the searing honesty brought about by Christ's blood and the unflinching courage brought about by Christ's water. Bring with you the tender intimacy of your own closeness to whatever it is and the profound awe of how it connects to the suffering of Christ. And dare to stay in that still place, a place of awe and intimacy, a place of water and blood, a place of grace and truth. This is the place of the *and*. Stay in the place of the *and*.

This *and* is the overlap between water and blood. It was a place the disciples couldn't occupy, which is why they scattered at this crucial moment and weren't around to witness the scene. They scattered because they wanted reality to be all water, and when they saw the blood, they turned to fear and despair. But the heart of being a Christian lies staying still right in this moment, where water and blood come out together. Being a Christian means remaining in the place where hope and suffering meet. This place, the place of water and blood, is the place where faith and fear overlap. It's maybe the most difficult place to be. But this is the place where the church was born. And this continues to be the place more than anywhere else where the church still belongs. The church is and always has been most truly itself not when soaring in success or when plunged in despair but when success and despair are mingled like water and blood. That's a place of conflict, horror and agony, but also of new birth, new community and new sources of life. This place has a name. It's called the foot of the cross.

18

Matched

When they came to the place that is called The Skull, they crucified Jesus there with the criminals, one on his right and one on his left. Then Jesus said, 'Father, forgive them; for they do not know what they are doing.' And they cast lots to divide his clothing. And the people stood by, watching; but the leaders scoffed at him, saying, 'He saved others; let him save himself if he is the Messiah of God, his chosen one!' The soldiers also mocked him, coming up and offering him sour wine, and saying, 'If you are the King of the Jews, save yourself!' There was also an inscription over him, 'This is the King of the Jews.'

One of the criminals who were hanged there kept deriding him and saying, 'Are you not the Messiah? Save yourself and us!' But the other rebuked him, saying, 'Do you not fear God, since you are under the same sentence of condemnation? And we indeed have been condemned justly, for we are getting what we deserve for our deeds, but this man has done nothing wrong.' Then he said, 'Jesus, remember me when you come into your kingdom.' He replied, 'Truly I tell you, today you will be with me in Paradise'. (Luke 23.33–43)

Let's imagine you're a king. You live in a dizzying castle, high up almost in the clouds, as all kings do. You have everything money can buy, everything influence can achieve, and everything power can claim. You're utterly independent: you don't need anyone.

But one reality changes everything. You love a lowly maiden – a person without fame or fortune or fine features or fair favour.

Your heart and soul and mind and strength are wrapped up in one question: How are you to win this lowly maiden's love?[1] You wrestle with this question. You toss and turn in your sleepless bed each night. You begin by thinking the ways kings do: you'll use your money, and influence, and power. You'll communicate to her, probably through an emissary, that she's your chosen one, and she'll be lifted from obscurity and brought to you like a banquet on a platter. How lucky for her. How magnanimous of you. How could she ever thank you?

But you're not a fool. You realize that this would provide you with her body, but not her soul, her will, or her heart. And you have no desire for the one without the others. You don't simply want her presence – you want her love. She would have no agency, no say in the question. She might be glad for the material blessings and the chance to advance her family's circumstances. She might be flattered, and even grateful. But none of these things are the same as love. She might learn to feign love – she might even convince herself for a season. But she'd never forget her origins and you'd never truly know if, on a level dance floor, she'd have chosen you. You'd remain a tyrant at worst or a benefactor at best.

So you come up with an idea: Plan B. You think, 'Let's take money out of the equation. Let's make sure she has wealth and acclaim before she knows why, and let's reassure her that they're a free gift and she won't lose them if she doesn't reciprocate my love. Let's raise her to my social level and so overcome the distance between us.' You begin to prepare a new castle in the air and all the possessions she could want. You get carried away with the excitement of having found a solution. But you soon realize this won't work. All she'll know of you is your wealth and grandeur. If she came to love you, you'd never really know why. She may love you out of gratitude or she may be delighted to be partnered with someone of her now

---

1 The story of the king and the maiden is adapted from Søren Kierkegaard, *Philosophical Fragments*, trans Howard V. and Edna H. Hong, Princeton University Press (1985).

exalted social standing. She may value the acclaim more than she values you. How would you ever really trust her?

But all is not lost. Reflecting on the problems in exalting the maiden's lowly status leads you to a third, much riskier plan. You could remove the trappings of majesty and adopt the clothes of poor man. Then, if she falls for you, you'll know it's not because of the power and wealth and influence and acclaim that you offer her. She'd truly be choosing you for the right reasons. There's a huge risk that she might reject your love, of course, but there isn't the same risk that she'll simply be using you, or you her.

Yet this third plan is swathed in deception, in disguise, in superficial appearance and ultimately in deceit. Sooner or later you're going to whip off your costume – or the mask will slip by itself. She thought she was loving you as an equal, but it would turn out you'd engineered the whole thing. How can real love begin with so giant a lie? How would she ever really trust you?

After countless restless nights you accept there's only one way to realize your desires. You must become like the one you love. You must become poor. It mustn't be a pretence, a subterfuge, a game, a sleight of hand. It must be for real. You must leave aside all the trappings of majesty and take up the life of a lowly person like the maiden that's taken possession of your heart. If she rejects you, well, that's the risk of love: being a king can't bypass or protect or subvert or shortcut the dangerous and delicate drama of enthralment and rejection, rapture or misery. There's no turning back.

Once you realize that this is the choice, there's no question: of course you'll do it. The trappings of majesty are nothing to you compared to the heart of your beloved. You'll risk it all, because in all this heartsearching you've made a vital discovery: that you only truly value what you can fully share.

And so you become a lowly servant. You're still a king: but no one who's used to meeting kings would recognize you. And your new form isn't a trick or a device: even if the maiden rejects you, you'll remain in the form you've become. There's no going back.

By now you'll have recognized this parable and its characters. The king in the parable is God. The lowly maiden is you and me. God could have remained aloof and beyond and outside our imagination and experience. But this is the central mystery, the heart of the wonder of grace. God loved us. We don't know why: we know it wasn't because we were beautiful, or worthy, or talented, or faithful. God just loved us.

God could have wooed us with gifts, and status, and luxury, and bribes. That was the king's first option. Maybe that's what the splendours of lakes, and waterfalls, and sunsets and flowers and butterflies are. But what kind of love do such things evoke in us? Gratitude, maybe, at best: wonder, quite possibly; but too often a will to possess, to subdue, to own. Alternatively God could have raised us up to be like gods ourselves. That was the second option. Maybe that's what happens when we fly beyond the speed of sound, when we clone human beings or obliterate a million people with a single bomb. Or there's the third option. God could have deceived us by pretending to be just like us before ripping the mask away when the going got uncomfortable.

But God didn't do any of these things. God in Christ set aside the trappings of majesty, and, while never ceasing to be a king, was voluntarily stripped of all the comforts and acclaim and protection we associate with the kingly picture of God. When he stood on trial before Pilate, when he hung naked on the cross, Christ had nothing left but his love of us. Why did God in Christ take this terrible, absurd risk, a risk almost bound to end in disaster? For no other reason than that God loved us, and wanted our genuine, heartfelt, uncomplicated love in return.

What a huge risk. And a risk that proved indescribably costly. The humble maiden rejected the love of the lowly servant. In Luke's description of the crucifixion, the leaders, the soldiers and the first thief all goad Jesus into going back to being the king in his castle, the king who can remove the mask and snap his fingers and use power and influence to fix everything. 'Come down from the cross', they say. 'Save yourself and us.' Only the second thief understands what almost everyone in the gospel story's missed: not only that this truly is the king, but also that this king's laid aside his majesty because of love for people just like these two between whom he's being crucified.

In many ways this is the climax of Luke's gospel, because here, at the moment of greatest rejection and greatest sacrifice and greatest agony, finally someone gets it. Finally someone realizes what this was all about; finally Jesus sees the glory of being loved in return. Paradise breaks through when for the first time someone looks at Jesus and sees not the opportunity of what Jesus can do *for* them but the sheer joy of his being *with* them. The poignancy of that discovery coming at the most utterly horrific moment in the history of the universe is the heart of the mystery of faith.

See what's happened here, in the wonder of the incarnation and in the horror of the cross: God hasn't stopped being a king; God's redefined what it means to be a king. If we're to look for true kingship, it's to be found among those who do as Christ has done; among those who set aside the power, acclaim and influence to discover love in true encounter. In Christ, in the crucified Lord, God is presenting us with a transformed picture of what it means to be a king.

Remember Jesus' encounter with the rich young ruler. We angst about whether Jesus' instructions to go, sell, give, come and follow really apply to us. But think about our parable of the king and the maiden: this is exactly what God does in Jesus – sheds all the trappings of majesty and sets off after us. Jesus is saying, you've got the question wrong: it's not 'What do I have to do to inherit eternal life?' The question is, says Jesus, 'Do you love me?' If you love me, do what I've done – set aside all other goals, seek me, and all other things will be added unto you. We want to settle for option 3 – to hold on to wearing the mask – to be able to switch back to our other life if our pursuit of God comes to grief. But that's not love. That's calculation. That's not the way God loves us. God has no plan B. God has put every egg in our basket. God has no mask.

In this astonishing moment we see that to be a king means not to be cosseted by privilege but to be stripped naked by love. And at this most precious, most painful, most intimate moment of loving and dying finally the lowly maiden responds to the king, and says, 'Jesus, remember me.' It's the only moment in all four gospels when anyone simply calls our Lord by his simple name, 'Jesus'. Not 'Son of God', not 'Christ', not 'Immanuel' or any of a hundred other names. Just this simple name, Jesus. Jesus, remember me. The king's stripped down to just that single name. In that simple, naked, name, humanity has finally, in the form of this dying thief, realized what the whole story, the whole parable of the Bible, was about.

And Jesus, in practically his last breath, says finally, poignantly, beautifully and definitively, 'Love has met its match. Together, today, you and I: on the cross, despite the cross, through the cross – we have glimpsed paradise.'

19

Crucified

The little boy used to bring home friends from school. They used to play in the living room. But his father began to notice that his son stopped bringing home friends to play. So he sat down on the stair with his son, the place where they would chat. He said, 'I've noticed you don't bring friends home to play anymore. Is it because of your mum?' His son nodded. 'Is it because of her hands?' His son nodded again. 'Let me tell you how your mum got those hands. One day when you were a very little boy she was next door and heard you screaming. You'd crawled into the fire. So she plunged her hands into the fire to get you out. But her hands were badly damaged. So when you see your mum's hands, you see how much she loves you.' A week or two later the father noticed his son started bringing friends home again. And one day he overheard his son say to a friend, 'You see my mum's hands? They show how much she loves me.'[1]

On Good Friday we see God's hands. And we see how much God loves us. God comes into our story and reveals not only the prisons others have put us in, but the prisons we have made for ourselves. The first kind of deliverance we call liberation, the second we call forgiveness. The first kind sets us free from oppression and death. The second kind sets us free from sin and stupidity. I want to explore today how the cross brings salvation in both senses.

---

1 I first heard this story from Jack Nicholls.

There's a tension that runs all the way through the Old Testament. On the one hand it seems Israel's major problem lies outside itself. The definitive story in the Old Testament is the story of the Exodus. This is the narrative of how Israel found itself in Egypt in a condition of slavery, with a hard-hearted Pharaoh impervious to the appeals of Moses to let his people go. This is an account of a people who'd done nothing to deserve their oppression. Like slaves snatched from West Africa and bundled into ships to come to North America in the seventeenth and eighteenth centuries, this was a people who had no part in their own enslavement. No law of nature or personal inadequacy had caused this: it was simply the hard-heartedness of their fellow human beings. God enters history to demonstrate a heart to set people free and a special love for Israel and the sore oppressed.

On the other hand it seems Israel's major problem lies inside itself. The definitive story may be the Exodus but the definitive location is the Jerusalem Temple. The Temple housed the Ark of the Covenant, the mercy seat where priests went to offer sacrifices to God to take away the people's sins. This was a people who were given freedom but forgot what to do with it. By turning to other gods, by neglecting the poor among them, by failing to keep the commandments, the people became estranged from God. They came to understand that they had gone into exile, and lost the Ark of the Covenant, precisely because they had strayed from God's ways. They built a new Temple, but it did not contain the Ark of the Covenant and so there was a sense that the regular sacrifices did not succeed in taking away sins.

The same tension that runs through the Old Testament runs through today's church and society. On the one hand it seems our major problems lie outside ourselves. Global hunger seems to be about a shortage of food, disease seems to be about shortage of medicine and cures, and the power of terrorism is that there seems to be no way in which reason can persuade it to stop. On the other hand it seems our major problems are of our own making. Climate change, species depletion, drug dependence and inequality are all problems that only a change in human behaviour can address.

As we contemplate Jesus' crucifixion, we see how Jesus overcomes both slavery and sin, both what others have done to us and what we have done to ourselves.

What others have done to us is represented in the story by Rome. Rome puts Jesus to death. Rome was in the habit of parading those they had defeated in battle through the streets in a triumphal march. Jesus likewise is paraded through Jerusalem, down the via dolorosa of humiliation, to Golgotha. Rome executes Jesus the way it executed political opponents. It puts an inscription over his head which says, 'The King of the Jews', both as an ironic taunt at this naked figure and as a warning for anyone who might similarly challenge Rome.

What we have done to ourselves is represented in the story by the Jerusalem Temple, and those who attend to its work. The Temple is an edifice built for sacrifice, but no one can see that the sacrifice that really matters is taking place before their eyes. The chief priests ironically summarize the whole gospel with their words 'He saved others; he cannot save himself' – but they're still obsessed with the idea of the Messiah not having to suffer, the idea that Jesus will bring transformation by pulling off a stunt and avoiding death at the last minute. They keep referring to Elijah, because Elijah was the prophet who never died, who went to heaven in a blaze of glory and was expected to scoop up any who were too good to die. The crucified God is looking down at the chief priests, but they can't see him. Jesus is of course their king, but it takes the sarcastic Romans to name him. Jesus is of course their new Temple, the one who really restores their relationship with God, but they tease Jesus by quoting back his words about rebuilding the Temple in three days.

And yet Jesus' crucifixion transforms Rome and transforms Jerusalem – transforms our outward oppression and our inward confusion, transforms the prison others put us in and the prison we put ourselves in.

Jesus' crucifixion transforms Rome by identifying Rome as Pharaoh's Egypt. 'When it was noon', Mark tells us, 'darkness came over the land until three in the afternoon.' The sun was gone for three hours. Go back to Exodus 10, in the heat of the contest between Moses and Pharaoh, and we read, 'Moses stretched out his hand towards heaven and there was dense darkness over all the land of Egypt for three days.' Pharaoh's Egypt worshipped the sun. Rome's Caesar was regarded as the sun. Egypt went dark for three days. Israel went dark for three hours. What is Mark telling us? He's telling us that the God of Israel had once put Pharaoh and his power in the shade and was now putting Rome and its power in the shade.

Then at the moment of Jesus' death his crucifixion transforms Jerusalem by identifying Jesus as the new Temple, the new sacrifice that finally takes away sins. 'Jesus gave a loud cry and breathed his last', we read, and then immediately 'the curtain of the Temple was torn in two, from top to bottom.' The Temple system, the ordering of Israel around the elaborate methods of propitiating God through timely sacrifice, the perpetual exile of the Jews from their true home at the heart of God, all this is suddenly over. Jesus is the full presence of God to us, and of us to God; he is the true place of reconciliation, and thus he is the new Temple that is the genuine place of encounter between us and God.

And this resolves the tension that runs all the way through the Old Testament. Does Israel's problem lie with external oppressors or with internal sin? Jesus' cross is God's judgement on both. The God who blots out the sun while Christ hangs on the cross is a God who can swat Rome aside with one sweep of the hand. The God who tears the curtain of the Temple in two while Christ swings from the tree is a God who sees Jesus' death as the sacrifice that finally brings sacrifice to an end. One part of the church says it's all about public politics and seems to believe only the first judgement matters. Another part of the church says it's all about personal morality and seems to believe only the second judgement matters. But the cross offers us both.

And then there's the big finish. The account doesn't finish with darkness at noon. It doesn't finish with the Temple's torn curtain. It finishes with the words of the Roman centurion, 'Truly this man was God's Son!' Why does it finish here? Because this summarizes everything that has gone before. It's the last word on oppression, because here is the Roman soldier, the one who is accustomed to calling his emperor the Son of God, realizing that here at the foot of the cross he was in the presence of the true Son of God. Just as when the sun went dark Pharaoh discovered that he was under the authority of a God far greater than his sun-god, so here the centurion discovers he's under the sovereignty of a Son of God greater than his Emperor. It's not just the last word on oppression, it's the last word on sin, because this Roman centurion is the man who had Jesus nailed to the cross. He's the man who killed Jesus. And here he is, at the moment of Jesus' death, realizing that the man he has killed is the Son of God. The cross has become the place where sins are forgiven.

So the cross is the last word on oppression and the last word on sin – but there's a hint of more even than that. The cross is the beginning of a new community. The chief priests thought they ran the community of God, but they have been exposed at the cross and condemned by their own words. The disciples thought they were becoming the new community of God, but at the cross they are nowhere to be seen. Instead we have a rag-tag new community of God. We had a hint of it in the dragooning of Simon of Cyrene to carry Jesus' cross. He has the same name as the first disciple and his sons' names, Alexander and Rufus, suggest he's not a Jew. He's the first of the new community. Then we have the centurion. He's an agent of the oppressing army who becomes the prophet who completes the gospel by announcing Jesus in the same words Mark uses in the very first line of his gospel – the Son of God. And then we have the faithful women disciples watching from afar. These are the ingredients from which God will make up the new community of the cross. They are the first to recognize the salvation Jesus brings. Jesus' cross has defeated oppression and forgiven sin. These are the first people to reap the benefits.

On Good Friday we see God's hands. Hands that formed us in creation, now stretched out in agony. Hands that, despite the agony, through the agony, deliver us from oppression and forgive us our sin. Hands that make a new community made up of foreigners and sinners and the socially excluded. A new community that has a place for us. On Good Friday we see God's hands. And we see how much God loves us.

20

Mocked

And when they had crucified him, they divided his clothes among themselves by casting lots; then they sat down there and kept watch over him. Over his head they put the charge against him, which read, 'This is Jesus, the King of the Jews.' Then two bandits were crucified with him, one on his right and one on his left. Those who passed by derided him, shaking their heads and saying, 'You who would destroy the temple and build it in three days, save yourself! If you are the Son of God, come down from the cross.' In the same way the chief priests also, along with the scribes and elders, were mocking him, saying, 'He saved others; he cannot save himself. He is the King of Israel; let him come down from the cross now, and we will believe in him. He trusts in God; let God deliver him now, if he wants to; for he said, "I am God's Son."' The bandits who were crucified with him also taunted him in the same way. (Matthew 27.35–44)

The film *Priest* introduces us to Fr Greg, a young and rather earnest Catholic priest, new to parish ministry. The film centres around two issues that torture and dominate his life. The first is that he's gay. Finding no legitimate outlet for this emerging part of his identity, he begins a secret relationship with a man he meets in a bar. The second is that he hears the confession of a teenage girl called Lisa. He learns that she is regularly being intimately assaulted by her father. Later the father comes to confession too, and the priest is horrified to realize that this man bears scarcely any remorse for what he is doing. The seal of the confessional means Fr Greg cannot communicate this information to anyone. But he struggles with that fact just as he wrestles with his own sexual identity. The power of his ability to pronounce or withhold forgiveness feels like nothing compared to his powerlessness to stop this terrible domestic tyranny.

The two traumas of his life come to a crisis at much the same time. He faces the humiliation of being arrested for behaving improperly with another man in a public place. He has the book thrown at him by his bishop, and is forced to leave the parish. Meanwhile the truth of Lisa's domestic ordeal suddenly comes to light. In a harrowing scene, Lisa's mother emerges from an angry crowd, and, squaring up to Fr Greg, with a tearful, bitter and unforgiving gaze, says to him, 'You knew.' Fr Greg has no idea what to say. Lisa's mother, now in disbelief and with her fury momentarily diverted from her husband and focused on her fragile and despised priest, says, witheringly and vengefully, 'You *knew.*'

This is the church Jesus died for. A church with lots of rules designed to keep us just and make us holy. Sometimes those rules are such that, try as we might, we can't keep them. Other times those rules are ones the keeping of which opens us to bitterness, fury and even hatred. The movie shows us both dimensions in the life of Fr Greg. Either way the church is exposed to public hatred and ridicule.

Public hatred and ridicule is the way the people of Jerusalem receive Jesus' crucifixion. Everything around the cross happens in threes. There've been three predictions of the passion earlier in the gospel. Then Jesus makes three predictions of who'll betray him – first Judas, then all the disciples, then Peter. Jesus prays three times in Gethsemane. Peter denies Jesus three times. After Jesus dies, three kinds of witnesses cluster around him: the soldiers, the women and Joseph of Arimathaea.

Here at the foot of the cross, there are three kinds of mockers. The first are the passers-by, who say, 'You who would destroy the temple and build it in three days, save yourself! If you are the Son of God, come down from the cross.' Then there are the chief priests, along with the scribes and elders, who say, 'He saved others; he cannot save himself. He is the King of Israel; let him come down from the cross now, and we will believe in him. He trusts in God; let God deliver him now, if he wants to; for he said, "I am God's Son."' Finally there are the bandits who are crucified with him who taunt him in the same way. This threefold taunting at the climax of Jesus' ministry echoes the threefold temptation at the outset of his ministry. In case there's any doubt of the connection, we get the same phrase used on both occasions – 'If you are the Son of God.' Both the devil and the mockers goad Jesus with his apparent inactivity. Surely a real divine being would offer fireworks and spectacle, not silent resignation? Come on Jesus, you can do better than this! How can you be the Messiah if you do nothing?

But the secret of the crucifixion scene is that there's many a true word spoken in jest. Between them this array of mockers gathered around Jesus succeed in summarizing and affirming pretty much every truth the gospel seeks to communicate. Let's take them one by one.

The passers-by say, 'You who would destroy the temple and build it in three days.' There's two ironies here. One is that this of course is exactly what Jesus is about to do – have his body destroyed and rebuilt in three days. The other is that the temple seemed the most indomitable feature of Israel's life. It had been destroyed once upon a time and it had taken a hundred years to rebuild it. It had been severely damaged later and had taken two hundred years to restore the second time. By the time Matthew's Gospel was written, it had been destroyed a third and final time ... But Jesus was very much alive. The mockers take for granted that the temple is permanent and Jesus is transitory. It turns out it's the other way round.

The passers-by continue, 'Save yourself.' But Jesus has already said, 'Those who want to save their life will lose it, and those who lose their life for my sake will find it.' There's almost nothing the mockers can say that Jesus hasn't anticipated in his public ministry.

Both the passers-by and the temple authorities say, 'If you are the Son of God', and 'He said, "I am God's Son."' But the ironic truth is, nowhere in the Gospel of Matthew does Jesus describe himself as the Son of God. The angel says it, the voice from the cloud says it, the centurion at the cross says it – but Jesus never says it. Somehow the mockers have intuited something Jesus has never said, and in trying to deride him they are in fact speaking a true word in jest.

Then the passers-by say, 'Come down from the cross.' But Jesus has already said, 'If any want to become my followers, let them deny themselves and take up their cross and follow me.' Once again, the mockers simply highlight the gospel Jesus has already proclaimed.

Of all the ironic statements at the foot of the cross, the most poignant are the words of the temple authorities, who say, 'He saved others; he cannot save himself.' This perfectly sums up the story the gospels tell. It's a double irony because the authorities think the joke's on Jesus, and that they're identifying the irony that Jesus can't do for himself what he can do for others. But meanwhile what they *can't* see is that the joke is finally on them, because first of all they've been drawn into identifying that Jesus has *indeed* saved others, a major acknowledgement for them to make, and secondly that there's something unique about Jesus that makes both him and his suffering different from others. And that pretty much sums up the gospel. Jesus saves us but at terrible cost to himself.

When you look at your life, whether you're a religious authority, a convicted criminal, or a passer-by, what do you see? Do you see a mockery of Jesus? That's what Fr Greg saw in the film. He saw a bunch of well-intentioned rules, designed to guide people on the right path and restore them when they went astray. But the rules designed to keep him on the path he found he couldn't keep, and the rules designed to restore his parishioners when they strayed seemed to make him powerless when he most needed strength. Lisa's mother pointed her finger at him when he was down, with all the uninhibited hatred the mockers aimed at Jesus on the cross. 'For a moment there I almost trusted you, I almost believed in you, you useless, pretentious, hypocritical creep.'

Our lives are indeed a perpetual mockery of Jesus. Our work is a parody of the self-sacrificial other-centred example of our Lord. Our relationships are a parody of the mutual-indwelling abiding trust of the Trinity. Our discipleship walk is a parody of the disciplined fraternal correction and compassionate forbearance Jesus commends. Our mission is a parody of humble and constant presence among the hungry, the naked, the stranger, the sick and the prisoner. Our congregational life is more like a squabble between self-righteous elder brothers than a welcome reception for prodigal sons. We are constantly at the foot of the cross, mocking the suffering Jesus.

But here's the irony. The more we mock, the truer Jesus becomes. The worse we fail, the greater grows our admiration and wonder at Jesus. The more pitiful our attempts to be faithful, the more necessary is our need for grace. The more we shout and scream at Jesus to come down from the cross, the more essential it is that he hangs there. The more we deride him and taunt him to save himself, the more we need him to save us. The more the church fails, the more we highlight the truth and urgent necessity of Jesus' person and message.

Christ's passion contains two great miracles. One is obvious, the one that God did – the miracle of resurrection. The other is more subtle, and it comes right at this moment. It is the miracle of what Jesus *didn't* do. He didn't come down from the cross. He stayed there. He outlasted our hatred and cruelty and enmity. After everything we could throw at him, physically and verbally, he was still there. His endurance demonstrated the love that will never let us go. His perseverance showed that nothing can separate us from the love of God. For ever after we can connect to God, not through our striving, but through Jesus' suffering, not through our longing, but through his lingering, not through our achieving, but through his abiding.

It's not the Jesus we want. We want the Jesus that comes

down from the cross, the Jesus that rights wrong, ends pain, corrects injustice, sends the wicked away empty, sets the record straight and makes all well with the world. We want answers, we want solutions, we want a technological Jesus who fixes the problems. And we want those problems fixed now. We want the Jesus that comes down from the cross. This Jesus will not come down from the cross. This Jesus bears all things, endures all things, and never ends ... This is not the God we want.

But it's the God we *need*. Oh how badly we need that God! Answers, explanations, solutions – they don't give us what we fundamentally need in the face of suffering and sin. What we need is love. What we need is a wondrous love through all eternity. Sure, what we *do* is show our inability to express that love. So we wash our hands like Pilate or run away like the disciples or lose patience like Judas or settle it with a sword like Peter. And so all the more what we *need* is a love that abides, that perseveres, that remains present to us, however bad things are, for however long it takes. What we *need* is a love that sticks around, a love that stays put, a love that hangs on. That's what the cross is. A love that hangs on.

I've taken countless funerals in working-class communities, and spent many hours trying to extract from mourners nuggets of wisdom and insight to give a personal touch to a funeral sermon. Of all those cameos, the most perennial is 'He was always there for you.' I've long pondered this ubiquitous phrase. Does it mean he was never out when you called? Does it mean simply you can't imagine life without him? I've come to the conclusion that it means what mattered was this man's presence, his wordless permanence, his abiding touch. 'He was always there for you.' I used to mock this phrase as a banal cliché that had no purchase in any specific personal quality or characteristic. But I've come to understand that this invariable description of the deeply mourned, 'He was always there for you', is none other than a description of the crucified God. We look at Jesus on the cross, and we say to one another, 'He's always there ... for *you*.'

The end of the film *Priest* contains the most moving scene I've witnessed in the cinema. Fr Greg returns to the parish after his time of humiliation and exile. The anger and hatred still smoulders in the neighbourhood and the parish. Lisa's mother's incandescent words, '*You knew*', are still ringing in his and our ears. Lisa hasn't been seen in the church since the truth about her household came to light. The senior priest, Fr Matthew, implores the congregation to receive Fr Greg back as their father in God. When it comes to receiving communion there are two stations for taking the bread, one from Fr Matthew, the other from Fr Greg. Every single worshipper at the service lines up to receive from Fr Matthew. Fr Greg stands alone, the body of Christ in his hands, totally shunned and visibly humiliated by the whole congregation. Seconds tick by and his isolation is ... crucifying. Somehow he finds the courage and defiance to continue to stand alone – to hang in there. And then slowly but purposefully one solitary figure shuffles forward and stands before him to receive communion. It's Lisa.

Their eyes meet as she receives the communion bread. Her eyes say, 'I know that you knew about my dad. But I know that you couldn't do anything about it. I understand your present powerlessness. I know it's because you believe in a greater power. You show me that by your courage in being present here right now. You're being crucified, but you're showing us a love that will not let us go.'

That's the irony of the cross. If Jesus had saved himself, he couldn't have saved us. His powerlessness shows us the endurance of God. Jesus hangs on the cross to show us the love that hangs on. Hang on to that love. It will never let you go.

Study Guide

This study guide provides a prayer and some prompts for discussion for each of seven weeks. The prompts are of two kinds. 'Tell about ...' invites participants to share recollections of events in their own lives. 'I wonder ...' invites them to speculate and imagine issues that don't have 'right' responses. These are not questions, and they don't have correct answers. They are ways of engaging deeply with the material in the book.

Week 1 – Introduction and Part 1

God of mercy, in Jesus you are with us always.
Be close to any who feel forsaken and alone.
Visit us in our place of abandonment
that we may know that nothing can separate us from you.
In Christ your son our Lord. Amen.

Tell about a time you thought, 'I only want to be with you.'
Tell about an occasion you felt profoundly without something or someone.
Tell about a time you felt the cross of Jesus really made sense to you.
I wonder what it was like for Jesus to feel forsaken.
I wonder with which of the main groups in the passion story you feel most at home.
I wonder if you feel you've been part of a community that was a 'context requiring an explanation'.

Week 2 – Part 2, Chapters 3–5

God of today and forever,
in Christ you emptied yourself of all but love.
Shape the life of your church,
that in gestures of grace and in costly holiness
you may be made known in your humility and your glory.
Through your crucified son. Amen.

Tell about a time you thought or said, 'Never again.'
Tell about an occasion you were tested.
Tell about a time you thought, 'Nothing is more important
than you.'
I wonder whether on the cross Jesus knew the Father would
provide.
I wonder whether you've ever not wanted to be told the
whole story.
I wonder if you've ever known someone who took terrible
punishment to protect others.

Week 3 – Part 2, Chapters 6–8

God of compassion and tenderness,
in Christ you say, 'Nothing is more important than you.'
By the power of your Holy Spirit,
so order our lives that we may be formed in the likeness
    of Jesus.
Be close to all who through suffering and oppression
are contorted into the shape of your son's crucified body.
Open our eyes that we may behold where your children are
    crucified today,
that we may see your face in theirs.
In the name of your son. Amen.

Tell about a time you felt you'd been set free.

Tell about an occasion that felt like a prefigurement of heaven on earth.
Tell about a time you saw someone being made a scapegoat.
I wonder whether you've ever been in awe of someone's faith.
I wonder whether there can be real truth in pain.
I wonder what it feels like to realize someone has saved your life.

Week 4 – Part 3, Chapters 9–11

Abiding God, you show us your face
in the heartbroken Father, the crucified son
and the comforting Spirit.
Give us grace to walk with your children
when they are bereft, miserable or exhausted.
Give us thankful hearts for those who have dwelt with us
when we could take it no more.
Embrace us in our times of grief,
that we may share with you in an eternity of glory.
In Christ your son. Amen.

Tell about a person who was your enemy but ended up saving you.
Tell about a time you've been furious with God.
Tell about a time you realized you'd used a theory to hide from a simple truth.
I wonder what it feels like to realize you are God's desire.
I wonder if your life has been captivated by *for* to the detriment of *with*.
I wonder how it feels to sense that there's more to the cross than you'd previously realized.

Week 5 – Part 3, Chapters 12–14

God of mystery, in the face of your crucified son
we see not anger but sorrow, not judgement but mercy.
Open our hearts to any who know only anger and judgement.
Seal us upon your arm and within your heart,
that we may know the freedom that lies beyond anger
    and judgement,
in the companionship of your Spirit.
In Christ our Lord. Amen.

Tell about a person you've known who seemed crazy but
actually saw the truth better than anyone.
Tell about a time you did something crazy.
Tell about a time you saw someone at breaking point.
I wonder what it feels like to have incompatible loyalties.
I wonder what it's like to know you're sealed upon God's arm.
I wonder what the dirty work really is for you today.

Week 6 – Part 4, Chapters 15–17

Faithful God, in your crucified son
we see that you are never finished with us.
Empty our hearts of all but love,
that we may respond with mercy in the face of injustice,
and may find our home beside those
on whom the world turns its back.
In Christ your son. Amen.

Tell about what time in your life you recall when you hear the
word 'finished'.
Tell about when you realized you had to let go of a previous
idea of what Christianity was.
Tell about a time you felt someone you were close to was
going in the wrong direction.

I wonder what made Judas do it.
I wonder if you've touched a dead body.
I wonder whether you're more likely to airbrush out the
water or the blood.

Week 7 – Part 4, Chapters 18–20

God of glory, your son knew shame and ridicule.
Be close to any who are humiliated today.
Lead us to place our hands in your wounds wherever we
    find them,
and give us strength to hang on to your love,
now and forever.
In Christ your son. Amen.

Tell about when you took a huge risk for something really
important.
Tell about when you have glimpsed paradise.
Tell about what your hands tell about what or who you love.
I wonder whether the fault lies mostly outside us or inside us.
I wonder what it's like to be ridiculed.
I wonder how you can hang on to a love that hangs on.

Printed in the USA
CPSIA information can be obtained
at www.ICGtesting.com
LVHW071319240923
758721LV00003B/10